Welcome

STIG ABELL
EDITOR, *TLS*

The brilliance of Shakespeare often resists explanation, not least because it has led to him being so ubiquitous. He has become part of the national furniture: just *there*, and so sometimes overlooked, even as anniversaries of his life come and go.

Here is a theory about why he was so exceptional. In him were combined two normally opposing forces: the necessary fluency of the jobbing professional; and the scintillating perspective of the genius. The voluble and expansive, as well as the minutely and perfectly crafted: in no figure before or since have these competing virtues been so unimprovably realized.

Shakespeare in the 1590s was the literary equivalent of a pop star, a writer whose work could be mined for sentimental *aperçus* with which to impress a lover; a proto-historical novelist, who gave a face and a force to English history. If he had died in 1598, he would have been remembered for *Romeo and Juliet, A Midsummer Night's Dream*, for Shylock and Falstaff. Of course, in the next two years he wrote *Henry V, Julius Caesar, As You Like It, Twelfth Night* and *Hamlet*: a run of excellence unmatched in history. Except perhaps by Shakespeare himself a few years later: *Othello, King Lear, Macbeth* and *Anthony and Cleopatra*....

This book is the *TLS*'s loving, scholarly, detailed and delighted tribute to William Shakespeare. We have been publishing essays and reviews about him for over a century, examining (and celebrating) his works more than those of any other writer. The purpose of the *TLS* has always been to publish each generation's best minds writing about the best minds of any generation. Shakespeare has always been both a subject and an inspiration.

Over the next hundred pages, you will find thoughts on Shakespeare's plays and poems. You will also find – in the spirit of his own eclectic mind – our selection of stories that have grown up around the man and his work. "Words, words, words", then, and we hope you enjoy every one of them.

Contents

Legend:
- Introduction
- Comedies
- Histories
- Tragedies
- Controversies
- Miscellanies

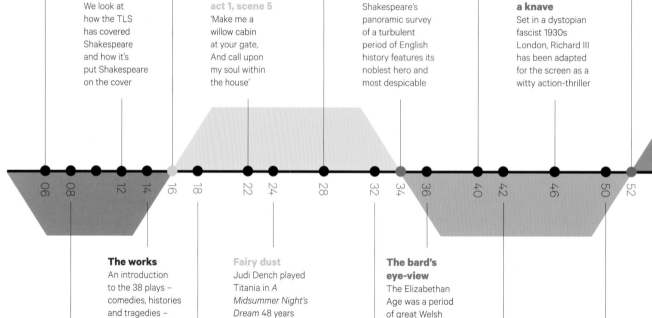

Man or monster
Coriolanus has always polarized opinion, its hero's frailties drawing ire and praise in equal measure

Critical responses
Critical responses to Shakespeare, the tragedian, and 'Macbeth' by Roy Fuller

Idle worship
Those who seek to deny Shakespeare's authorship of more than 30 plays are driven to strange expedients

All is but toys
We go back to the future to see what computer-games technology made of *Macbeth* in 1986

Sonnet
'Sonnet 103', which begins, 'My mistress' eyes are nothing like the sun...'

Doctor in the house
Television series stars David Tennant and Patrick Stewart headed the cast in a modern-dress staging of *Hamlet*

Shall I compare thee?
An exhibition of Shakespeare portraits set off a chain of responses from Bard scholars

Greasepaint and oils
Shakespeare productions and the stage became popular subjects for late nineteenth-century painters

Shakespeare's London
Our guide to the capital's landmarks – and theatres – that the Bard helped put on the map

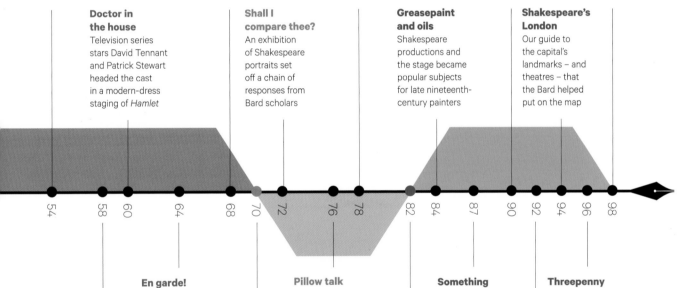

54 — 58 — 60 — 64 — 68 — 70 — 72 — 76 — 78 — 82 — 84 — 87 — 90 — 92 — 94 — 96 — 98

En garde!
Six Shakespeare devotees put on their bookies' hats to discuss the odds of Hamlet outfencing Laertes

Pillow talk
Scholars do gentle battle over the 'primarily homosexual context' of Shakespeare's Sonnets

Something rocking in Denmark
Over 20,000 pieces of music have been penned in tribute to Shakespeare

Threepenny Lear
Bertolt Brecht reveals himself to be a firm fan of the Bard's keen sense of time and place

Julius Caesar, act 3, scene 1
'Thou art the ruins of the noblest man That ever lived in the tide of times...'

Controversies
Shakespeare's sexual orientation, physical appearance and authorship have long been a source of controversy

Miscellanies
Shakespeare lives on, in song, paint, computer games and his influence on others

This be the verse
TS Eliot praises Shakespeare's appetite for words and recognises his debt to Montaigne

Credits

Editor
Stig Abell

Issue editor
Michael Caines

Consulting editor
Tiffanie Darke

Creative director
Darren Smith

Art director
Sachini Imbuldeniya

Design
Lee Martin,
Valentina Verc

Sub-editors
George Berridge,
Sabhbh Curran,
Lucy Dallas,
Joseph Furey,
Andrew Irwin,
Thea Lenarduzzi,
Catharine Morris,
Mika Ross-Southall,
Adrian Tahourdin

Picture research
Matthew Glynn,
Martin Smith,
Eithne Staunton,
Annalee Mather

Editorial assistant
Jennifer Hahn

Cover illustration
Valentina Verc

TLS

Copyright © The Times Literary
Supplement Limited 2016. The Times
Literary Supplement Limited: 1 London
Bridge Street, London SE1 9GF. Registered
in England. Company registration number:
935240. VAT no: GB 243 8054 69.

Contributors

Bertolt Brecht (1898–1956).
One of the great playwrights of
the twentieth century, Brecht was
the author of *The Threepenny
Opera*, *The Resistible Rise of Arturo
Ui* and *The Caucasian Chalk Circle*.
John Willett, a leading English expert
on this German writer, was deputy
editor of the *TLS* during the 1960s.

Julia Briggs (1943–2007)
A literary scholar with a wide range
of interests, including Renaissance
literature, children's books and
Virginia Woolf. She was awarded an
OBE for her services to English
literature shortly before her death.

Iain Crichton Smith (1928–1998)
A Scottish poet who wrote verses
in both Gaelic and English, and
was prolific and versatile in prose,
too. His *New Collected Poems*
appeared in 2010.

Katherine Duncan-Jones
A retired Fellow of Somerville
College, Oxford, and an eminent
scholar of early modern English
literature. She edited *Shakespeare's
Sonnets* (1997) and has written
books about Shakespeare's
"ungentle life" (2010) and *Portraits
of Shakespeare* (2016).

TS Eliot (1888–1965)
One of the towering figures of
twentieth-century literature. He
was the author of the seminal
modernist poem *"The Waste Land"*
(1922), an influential critic who
wrote regularly for the *TLS*, and
a playwright. He received the Nobel
Prize in Literature for 1948.

Barbara Everett
A retired Fellow of Somerville
College, Oxford. A veteran contributor
to the *TLS*, her books include

*Poets in Their Time: Essays on
English Poetry from Donne to Larkin*
(1986) and *Young Hamlet: Essays on
Shakespeare's Tragedies* (1989).

Juliet Fleming
An associate professor of English
at New York University, and the
author of *Graffiti and the Writing
Arts of Early Modern England*
(2001) and *Cultural Graphology:
Writing after Derrida* (2016).

Roy Fuller (1912–1991)
Best known as a dryly eloquent poet,
although he also wrote novels,
memoirs and much else besides. He
was Professor of Poetry at Oxford
University 1968–1973, and his
Selected Poems appeared in 2012.

David Hawkes
A teacher at Arizona State University.
His books include *Milton: a Hero of
Our Time* (2009) and *Shakespeare
and Economic Criticism* (2015).

Peter Holland
A distinguished Shakespearean
scholar at the University of Notre
Dame, who edits the academic
journal *Shakespeare Survey*. He has
also written about Restoration drama,
Chekhov and English pantomime.

RD Lancaster
A poet who was published irregularly
in the *TLS* between the 1950s and
1980s. Born in 1922, he served in
the Royal Artillery during the Second
World War, and seems to have
published little – or maybe nothing
at all – in book form.

John Middleton Murry
(1889–1957)
Husband of the writer Katherine
Mansfield and the editor of her work
after her death, Murry wrote

extensively for the *TLS*, over five
decades. He also published books on
subjects ranging from Shakespeare, his
friend DH Lawrence and Dostoevsky
to Communism, pacifism and religion.

Michael Pennington
An actor and director, his books
include *Hamlet: a User's Guide* (1996),
Twelfth Night: a User's Guide (2000)
and *Sweet William: Twenty Thousand
Hours with Shakespeare* (2012).

Lois Potter
A distinguished literary scholar
whose books include the Arden
edition of *The Two Noble Kinsmen*
(1996), a study of *Othello* in
performance (2002) and *The Life
of William Shakespeare* (2012).
She retired in 2008 as a professor of
English at the University of Delaware.

Nicholas Robins
Works at Shakespeare's Globe.
His books include *Walking
Shakespeare's London* (2004) and,
as co-editor, *The Oxford Guide to
Literary Britain and Ireland* (2008).

Emma Smith
A professor of Shakespeare
Studies and a Fellow of Hertford
College, Oxford, she is the author
of *Shakespeare's First Folio: Four
Centuries of an Iconic Book* (2016)
and the co-author *of Thirty Great
Myths about Shakespeare* (2012).

Brian Vickers
Knighted for his services to literary
scholarship in 2008, he has written for
the *TLS* since 1970, on subjects such
as rhetoric and literary theory. He has
edited the works of Francis Bacon and
John Ford, and written books on
Shakespeare including *Shakespeare,
Co-Author: A Historical Study of
Five Collaborative Plays* (2002).

Sonnet 18

Shall I compare thee to a summer's day?
Thou art more lovely and more temperate:
Rough winds do shake the darling buds of May,
And summer's lease hath all too short a date:
Sometime too hot the eye of heaven shines,
And often is his gold complexion dimmed;
And every fair from fair sometime declines,
By chance, or nature's changing course, untrimmed;

But thy eternal summer shall not fade,
Nor lose possession of that fair thou ow'st,
Nor shall death brag thou wander'st in his shade
When in eternal lines to time thou grow'st.
So long as men can breathe or eyes can see,
So long lives this, and this gives life to thee.

ILLUSTRATION: VALENTINA VERC

Shakespeare's Sonnets were first published in 1609 with a long poem called "A Lover's Complaint". There were 154 of these fourteen-line poems in which love and sex figure prominently, but in which may also be found piety, parody, politics and a couple of Greek epigrams paraphrased (see "Pillow Talk", pages 76-77). The well-known Sonnet 18 playfully makes a comparison between its addressee and a "summer's day" – the final point in the addressee's favour being that the poem itself is lasting testimony to his or her loveliness.

ESSAYS

A life lived in one man's light

The theatrical career of this actor, director and writer has been bookended by the life and death of Shakespeare. Here, he imagines the questions he would ask and the thanks he would give if he met the playwright tomorrow

AUTHOR: MICHAEL PENNINGTON

April 23, 1964 marked the 400th anniversary of Shakespeare's birth – and the beginning of my career. I was a supernumerary in *The Wars of the Roses* with the RSC, and I could stand on the terrace outside the Green Room (homemade pies and crumbles in those days, nothing rotating at 750 watts), and look across the Avon at the pavilion that housed Richard Buckle's huge Shakespeare Exhibition. It was mostly recorded speeches, some lifesize cut-outs of the characters and laborious guesses as to what Shakespeare's Stratford-upon-Avon might have felt like, and it was heavily criticized. Meanwhile I was thinking what luck was mine to be making my debut as part of the live event, albeit as the fifteenth foot soldier from the left.

On the same day fifty-two years later I marked the 400th anniversary of Shakespeare's death by playing a matinee and evening as King Lear on tour in Northampton. Between the two performances I planted a mulberry tree in Abington Park, near the Peacock Aviary. King James I, a champion of mulberry trees, inspired Shakespeare, keen to honour the birth of his first granddaughter Elizabeth, to plant one in his garden in Stratford. Elizabeth survived the Civil War, married well and moved into her husband's family home in Abington Park. A century after that, the aptly named Thomas Sharpe cut down Shakespeare's tree and started selling off bits of it as mementoes; at that moment, the Shakespeare knick-knack industry was born.

Naturally, now that I've noticed this odd congruity between my

RIGHT
Michael Pennington, playing King Lear, plants a kiss on the head of Gloucester (Pip Donaghy) at the Royal & Derngate, Northampton, in April 2016

working life (thus far) and Shakespeare's mortal one, I've not been slow to tell anybody who'll listen, as if it gave me special privileges. In that, I'm only doing what many of us do, all the time – trying to take a selfie with Shakespeare. It is an odd experience to be spoken to intimately throughout your life by someone so anonymous. We badly want to be in touch with him, or at least to learn something more; the anxiety is palpable and the hope rather forlorn.

The big news this year was that ground-penetrating radar suggests that Shakespeare's grave in Stratford may have been ransacked and his skull moved to Bearley Church up the road. The excitement has only been dampened a little by the discovery that the suspect skull there has turned out to be that of a woman

in her seventies. The Stratford schoolroom where Shakespeare sat for twelve hours a day, six days a week, with a small break for bread and beer, opened to the public at last. In Somerset House an exhibition called By Me William Shakespeare offered the first sighting of Shakespeare's will for forty years, signed in his faltering hand (he had scrivener's palsy at the end, and no wonder).

At the British Library you could have marvelled at the headdress worn by Vivien Leigh when she played Titania in 1937 at the Old Vic. Among those who came to the show were the two young princesses, Elizabeth and Margaret: Elizabeth was so fascinated to see how the fairies flew that she almost fell out of the box. Robert Helpmann (Oberon) and Vivien Leigh were introduced in the interval, but while they were bowing and curtseying their wire headdresses became entangled and had to be pulled apart by the royal party, much to the princesses' amusement.

What there wasn't anywhere was a bitchy diary entry about what a pain Richard Burbage was to write for, or how hard it was to find the right ending for Cymbeline. Or any suggestion as to why Shakespeare wrote a series of comedies directly after his son's death; or what put it in his mind, when Charmian kills herself in *Antony and Cleopatra*, to have her say, with inexplicable brilliance, on her last breath "Ah, soldier!" when there is no significant soldier about.

Shakespeare books keep bucketing out each year, their focus increasingly biographical, as if well-researched minutiae – a signature on a document here, a brush with the law there – were a better way of getting close than the texts and his contemporaries' adulation. Yet Shakespeare's fabled secretiveness, compared to the

rock'n'roll manners of Christopher Marlowe and the grandiosities of Ben Jonson, remains unbreached, the best guess being that it was the lifelong result of his Catholic upbringing under a Protestant regime that bankrupted his father. James Shapiro in 1599 and Charles Nicholl in *The Lodger: Shakespeare on Silver Street* have written brilliantly about him by describing not the man himself but the world he moved through and the events that bore down on him, leaving a Shakespeare-shaped hole in the middle for the reader to fill.

Every time I do a Shakespeare play I wonder what he was like and come to a different conclusion. Currently, I think he was quite short and had a slow smile but a sudden, high-pitched laugh; that among playwrights he was,

ARENAPAL

BELOW
Michael Pennington in rehearsal for a 1988 production of *Henry V* at Sadler's Wells studios

in his manner, more like Stephen Poliakoff than David Hare, and among actors that he resembled Tom McGovern, who is playing Kent with me – nimble, industrious and friendly, only Tom has better teeth and is not afraid of the Plague. What I never imagine is anything like the Droeshout engraving, which makes Shakespeare's forehead very big, as if a child had been asked to draw a picture of a brainy man; or the porcine one in Stratford Church, from which you can only deduce that you wouldn't want to cross him if you were a tenant farmer on his land.

I've also wondered about meeting him, and thought it would be a more humorous version of meeting God. On the other hand it might be frustrating. I might find myself chasing this preoccupied figure as he weaved his practised way along Bankside or through the fields to Charlecote – I'm sure he suffered from the disease Chekhov called autobiographobia. Still, I'll have my questions ready, and rather than gushing I would show a knowing curiosity and even rib him a little about some imperfections, since after all that is an aspect of love. I'm sure he was someone who hung about and listened as much as he read, and I'd want to know in which Warwickshire pub he first heard a Shallow and Silence talking about the price of ewes and the inevitability of death in the faltering rhythms of the elderly, shying away from the unknown into their memories of youthful virility. I'd ask him to confirm my belief that when he thought of the citizens in *Coriolanus* as being no surer...

> Than is the coal of fire upon the ice,
> Or hailstone in the sun

he was on his way to the funeral of his brother Edmund at St Saviour's in Southwark, announced by the "fore-noon knell of the great bell" which had cost him twenty shillings to hire; noting as he walked across the frozen Thames that opportunistic shopkeepers had lit fires on the thick ice to keep warm and do business. He went on to memorialize this harmless brother by using his name for the villain in *King Lear*. Also in *Coriolanus*, we now know that while the First Citizen denounces noblemen who hoard grain that should be feeding hungry mouths, that was the very thing that Shakespeare himself was doing in Stratford. And as for the mulberry tree, I'd suggest to him that when Timon of Athens announces that he has a tree growing in his close when he is living in an improvised shelter on a deserted heath where nothing grows, his author had perhaps paused, looked up from his desk for inspiration, and seen it in front of him, in his garden at Stratford.

More sternly I would ask him why he only ever made up two original stories in his whole career; and whether the perfunctoriness of some of the plays' endings has to do with having to get on with the company jig that concluded even the darkest of tragedies. I might have to lodge an affectionate complaint about his Act Fours, when the accelerating action often stops either for repetition of earlier jokes or for a series of parleys

I'd thank him for MAKING us all TALENTED, so that we can see what he MIRACULOUSLY sees

MICHAEL PENNINGTON

before the battle. Or the innuendoes, so often about that great comedy subject, the sexually transmitted disease. I'd have to say we're not so thrilled these days by some of the jokes – by Portia shuddering at the thought of being married to a black man; by the French Princess in *Henry V* pronouncing English words so that they sound dirty. For these reasons, I feel bound to let him know that some people believe he should not be on the new National Curriculum.

Why would I do all this? Because I want him to know that I'm on to him. But now, as he begins to bristle, I tell him some of the unexpected things that make me love him. By what miracle did it occur to him that the merest servant in Timon should describe the dispersal of his colleagues as a departure "Into this sea of air" or to give a hired Murderer in *Macbeth* lines as beautiful as...

The west yet glimmers with some streaks of
day;
Now spurs the lated traveller apace
To gain the timely inn.

And as for timelessness, I'd reassure him that there is every sign in 2016 that he was right to predict that "humanity must perforce prey on itself, / Like monsters of the deep" and that the poor naked wretches in Lear's storm are to be found in the Calais Jungle. I'd pay tribute to the rolling thunder of the language itself, its fantastic twists and foibles; its buoyancy and good humour and neighbourliness. I'd thank him for making us all talented, so that we can see what he miraculously sees, whether in the natural world, in human eccentricity or the heart of darkness. And above all the alchemy whereby a simple idea is transformed by his sense of cadence, tension and

release, harmony and syncopation, into something that embeds our unexpressed feelings in a musical pattern that, now we hear it, we always knew was there. I'd praise him for two of the finest small love affairs in the canon, between Falstaff and Doll Tearsheet in *Henry IV* and between Margaret and Suffolk in *Henry VI* – the first as tender and the second as passionate as *Romeo and Juliet*, and likewise based on the woman's perception that it's best to part quickly when the game is up: it's the goodbyes that are agony. I'd pay tribute to the famous moment when Lear in his madness tells the Fool they'll go to supper in the morning and the Fool replies that he'll go to bed at noon – lines whose real beauty is in their sanity: they've been out on the heath all night and had no supper, so it would obviously be better to have a nap now, then eat something, and go back to bed later the next morning. I can see how he's done it – how the disyllables of the first line counterpoint the conclusive monosyllables of the second to make it unforgettably sad as well. Lear continues the play talking with the greatest simplicity of undone buttons, garden watering cans and becoming like a man of salt in his grief; of his 268 words in his final scene with the dead Cordelia, 232 are monosyllables.

This is probably the moment Shakespeare would shrug his shoulders and say he can't remember any of it – like an actor asked why he did some piece of stage business in a performance thirty years ago. As I feel what Leontes in *The Winter's Tale* calls a great gap of time re-opening between us, I call after him to thank him for having invented most of what we take for granted in the theatre, and for firing up five generations in my own time – including a couple before mine and a couple after – to exceptional efforts to do him as proud as we possibly can. ∎

ARCHIVE

We've got it covered

The leading international weekly for literary culture, the *TLS* chalked up its century 12 years ago. Here, we look at some of the editions that it has dedicated to Shakespeare

April 22, 2016; Issue 5899

October 30, 1992; Issue 4674.

February 4, 2005; Issue 5314

September 4, 2015; Issue 5866

August 10, 2012; Issue 5706

August 12, 2011; Issue 5654

March 23, 2001; Issue 5112.

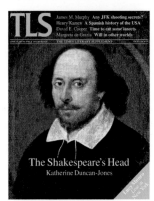

April 25, 2014; Issue 5795

October 9, 2015; Issue 5871

August 17, 2007; Issue 5446.

January 02, 2004; Issue 5257.

May 12, 2000; Issue 5067.

August 13, 2010; Issue 5602

April 18, 1997; Issue 4907

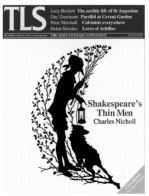

December 13, 2013; Issue 5776

July 27, 1967; Issue 3413

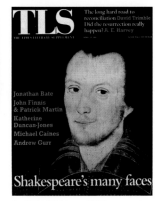

April 18, 2003; Issue 5220

The works

What Shakespeare wrote, when he wrote it, and why you should read it

1. THE TWO GENTLEMEN OF VERONA
Two friends fall in love with the same woman, Silvia, despite one of them, Proteus, having exchanged vows of love with Julia, from Verona. Proteus betrays his friend, who is banished by Silvia's father after his plan to elope with her comes out. Julia, disguised as a man, follows her beloved to Milan, where matters are more or less satisfactorily resolved for all.

2. THE TAMING OF THE SHREW
This controversial comedy depicts Petruchio and his brutal taming of his shrewish wife Katherine. Casting everything in an ironic light is a framing device, in which the play is acted before a drunken tinker made to think he's a lord.

3. HENRY VI PART 2
The second part of the *Henry VI* trilogy was written first. While various nobles vie for power, the Duke of York encourages a clothier called Jack Cade to lead a rebellion. Cade is killed, but it is merely the prelude to York's victory at St Alban's, thus initiating the War of the Roses.

4. HENRY VI PART 3
This play covers the death of the Duke of York, although there is more betrayal and fighting to come after that. Henry VI laments the fate of his violently divided kingdom, in a speech that is followed by a son bringing in the body of the father he has killed in battle – and a father bringing in the body of the son he has likewise killed.

5. HENRY VI PART 1
The *Henry VI* plays are likely the result of a collaboration with a fellow playwright. *Part One* takes the story from the death of Henry V through to his son's marriage to Margaret of Anjou. There is an iconic scene in which Richard Plantagenet, later the Duke of York, and the Duke of Somerset pick white and red roses as their insignia as rival claimants to the throne.

6. RICHARD III
A brilliantly straightforward play depicting the rise of Richard, Duke of Gloucester, to the throne, and what is required to remove the rivals in his way. It is capped by the instigation of a new dynasty under the first of the Tudors: Henry VIII-to-be.

7. TITUS ANDRONICUS
An extraordinarily bloody tragedy, it features, among other things, the rape and mutilation of Lavinia, Titus's daughter, and a scene in which this Roman general serves his enemy Tamora, Queen of the Goths, the remains of her sons baked in a pie.

8. THE COMEDY OF ERRORS
This energetic take on the Roman play Menaechmi by Plautus involves two masters, Antipholus of Syracuse and Antipholus of Ephesus, who are twins, and their two servants, Dromio of Syracuse and Dromio of Ephesus, who also happen to be twins. Cue confusion.

9. LOVE'S LABOUR'S LOST
The King of Navarre and his courtiers vow to devote themselves to their studies and forego the company of women. But the Princess of France and her three ladies turn up. Absurdities arise as everyone falls in love. The play ends with a turn away from comedy: a sequel, "Love's Labour's Won", seems to be promised.

10. A MIDSUMMER NIGHT'S DREAM
The comedy leads four Athenians into a wood, and intertwines their story with a spat between Oberon and Titania, the fairy king and queen, and the mishaps of a group of actors – principally Bottom the Weaver, who is magically given the head of an ass. The play combines knockabout silliness with a send-up of theatre itself.

11. RICHARD II
Written wholly in verse, *Richard II* marks a turn towards an earlier period in English history. Richard is given some of the finest speeches in the whole canon, but it is his uncle John of Gaunt who delivers those famous lines about "This blessed plot, this earth, this realm, this England".

12. ROMEO AND JULIET
Two "star-crossed" lovers are divided by a feud between their families, the Montagues and the Capulets. A work of unforgettable lyricism, it is also a tragedy of unhappy accidents, as a crucial letter miscarries and Romeo's friend Mercutio dies in a duel with Juliet's cousin Tybalt.

13. THE MERCHANT OF VENICE
If this comedy is best known for Shylock, the Jewish moneylender who goes to court in an effort to take a pound of flesh from the merchant Antonio, it has many other glories. In fact, Portia – who, in the guise of a lawyer, famously begs Shylock to show mercy – has nearly twice as many lines as him. Shylock, once played as a comic buffoon, is now seen as an almost tragic figure.

14. KING JOHN
In this verse play that scrutinizes the workings of power, the King is caught between political factions in a struggle that leads to war with France and to the deaths of both himself and his nephew who has a claim to the throne. It's a sardonic commentary on history that places Richard I's bastard son at the heart of the drama.

15. HENRY IV PART 1
Having usurped the throne, Henry IV is consumed by guilt, and wishes to expiate his crime by going on a crusade to the Holy Land. Unrest in Scotland and Wales intervenes, however, and there is the unruliness of the King's son Prince Hal, who prefers the company of the roguish Falstaff to life at Court. Rebellion against the Crown leads to the Battle of Shrewsbury, where Hal distinguishes himself.

16. THE MERRY WIVES OF WINDSOR
Supposedly written at the request of Elizabeth I, this delightful comic romp revives one of Shakespeare's most popular characters, Sir John Falstaff, putting the fat knight at the heart of the action, in order to expose and punish him for courting two wealthy married women at the same time.

17. HENRY IV PART 2
The least typical, perhaps the most underrated of the history plays, it threatens to repeat the action of the first Henry IV play, but includes a meditation on age and comic business with Falstaff. The closing acts are remarkable for the dialogue between the dying Henry and his heir, and Falstaff's public humiliation.

18. MUCH ADO ABOUT NOTHING
Set in Messina in the aftermath of military conflict, this is another favourite,

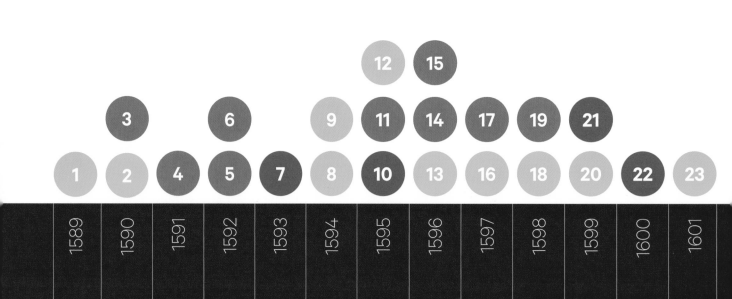

12 15

3 6 9 11 14 17 19 21

1 2 4 5 7 8 10 13 16 18 20 22 23

1589 1590 1591 1592 1593 1594 1595 1596 1597 1598 1599 1600 1601

largely due to the witty sparring between Benedick and Beatrice, and the plot their friends devise to bring them together. A darker, parallel plot is devised by Don John to separate Beatrice's cousin from Benedick's friend – it takes the local watch, led by the clownish Dogberry, to reveal the truth and save the day.

19. HENRY V

Shakespeare here turns his focus from domestic politics to war between England and France. King Henry's famous speeches during the siege of Harfleur and Agincourt have been celebrated as patriotic pieces of poetry in their own right, while the military action is offset by the English King's courtship of the French princess, Katharine.

20. AS YOU LIKE IT

This is the play that gave the world "All the world's a stage… ." Upheavals at court lead various characters to seek refuge in the Forest of Arden. Here Duke Senior, the ruler of the realm, hears out the ruminations of the melancholy Jacques, while Orlando adorns the trees with awful verses declaring his love for Rosalind, who is also there, disguised as a man.

21. JULIUS CAESAR

Despite its title, this tragedy kills off Caesar midway, shifting its focus to the fates of those who conspired against him: Brutus and the ambitious Cassio, against whom Mark Antony rouses the people of Rome ("Friends, Romans, countrymen, lend me your ears").

22. HAMLET

A story of revenge – as Prince Hamlet seeks retribution for the murder of his father by his uncle, who also marries his mother – the play expands to become so much more than that – it gives us Hamlet's soliloquies, including the most famous of all ("To be or not to be…"), Ophelia's madness and the most well-known skull in English literature: "Alas, poor Yorick! I knew him, Horatio…"

23. TWELFTH NIGHT

In Illyria, Orsino sends the boy Cesario to woo a mourning lady, Olivia, on his behalf. Only Olivia falls in love with Cesario – and Cesario is not a boy at all, but a woman called Viola in disguise. Meanwhile, Olivia's kinsman Sir Toby Belch and her unsuitable suitor Sir Andrew Aguecheek seek revenge against her steward Malvolio. The play strikes a fine balance between farce and melancholy.

24. TROILUS AND CRESSIDA

A bleak take on the poem by Chaucer of the same name, the play takes place in the context of Homer's *Iliad*. The Greeks are besieging Troy, while Pandarus plays the role of a go-between in the relationship of Trojan prince Troilus and Cressida – only for her to be exchanged for a Trojan prisoner of war. No, things do not end well.

25. MEASURE FOR MEASURE

Set in Vienna, this is a chillingly cynical piece of work about power and sex.

The Duke leaves Angelo, a deputy, in charge of the city, but remains there in disguise rather than going abroad as he has suggested. When a nun pleads for her brother's life, Angelo abuses his power by demanding that she sleep with him in exchange for a pardon. Further secrets are exposed and justice might seem to be done – to the Duke, if not to the audience.

26. OTHELLO

The perfect tragedy of jealousy, in which the heroic, Moorish soldier of the title is manipulated by his ensign, the wicked Iago, into believing his wife has been unfaithful to him. The action moves to Cyprus, where Othello's focus is meant to be on an external enemy, the Turks, but instead the plot hurtles towards a calamity entirely of one man's making.

27. KING LEAR

Majestically bleak, this play, one of the great tragic works in world literature, concerns the aged King Lear's division of the kingdom of Britain between his daughters, an act which goes wrong from the moment he rejects Cordelia, the most virtuous of them, and allots her share to her treacherous siblings, Goneril and Regan. Their subsequent treatment of him drives him into madness.

28. ALL'S WELL THAT ENDS WELL

Helena, a doctor's daughter, is in love with Bertram, Count of Rousillon. After Helena cures the King of a disease, she is granted her request to marry Bertram,

against his wishes. He goes off to war and leaves her a paradoxical challenge: he will only accept her as his wife when she has a ring from his finger and a child of his body. By the end of this "problem play", she has found a way of solving that paradox.

29. TIMON OF ATHENS

In this powerful satire on hypocrisy and greed, likely to have been co-written with Thomas Middleton, Timon's generosity to his friends turns to bitterness when they fail to come to his aid when he falls abruptly on hard times. He curses the city and leaves it – only to discover gold out in the wilderness. Only this source of wealth serves his newly misanthropic spirit.

30. MACBETH

Ambition awakens in Macbeth, a Scottish general for whom three witches, after a battle, prophesy great things. His wife urges him on, even as they host King Duncan in their castle. Shakespeare vividly depicts Macbeth's qualms about the murder he commits, but also his ruthlessness in holding on to power.

31. ANTONY AND CLEOPATRA

This tragedy is set at a point when the two lovers (and rulers) of the title are already legendary figures. Cleopatra is Shakespeare's most magnificent female character; Antony is induced to marry Octavia, the sister of a fellow triumvir of Rome, but cannot resist Cleopatra's "infinite

variety". War ensues, the outcome is certain – but there is much more to this, a meditation on human frailties behind the myths.

32. PERICLES

Pericles, Prince of Tyre, puts his life in danger by solving a riddle, wins a joust and loses his wife and daughter in a storm at sea. Despite everything Fate can throw at them, the family is reunited.

33. CORIOLANUS

A last Roman play, which tells of what happens when a military hero tangles with popular politics. The proud Caius Marcius is dubbed Coriolanus for his actions in battle against the Romans' enemies, the Volscians, at the city of Corioli – yet his brief political career in Rome ends in his exile and his turning to the Volscians. This doesn't go so well, needless to say.

34. THE WINTER'S TALE

A romance of extraordinary beauty, in which Leontes, King of Sicilia, falls into a jealous rage concerning a friend and his wife. The play turns from tragedy to comedy, however, and the intense drama at court gives way to bucolic scenes in Bohemia. The play includes perhaps the most celebrated stage direction of all time: "Exit, pursued by a bear".

35. CYMBELINE

This romance set in ancient Britain focusses on King Cymbeline's daughter Innogen, who is secretly married to a commoner rather than her stepmother's

cloddish son. Yet the play expands to take in an invasion by the Roman army and the discovery of the King's sons in the wilds of Wales. It's as ridiculous and wonderful as it sounds.

36. THE TEMPEST

Prospero, the banished Duke of Milan and sorceror, causes a shipwreck in order to regain his dukedom. Prospero's daughter Miranda has grown up in his care, knowing only the island, and it is she who utters the famous phrase "O brave new world" on seeing other people for the first time.

37. THE TWO NOBLE KINSMEN

A tragicomedy co-written with John Fletcher. The "kinsmen" are cousins, Palamon and Arcite, who are imprisoned in Athens after a battle, and fall in love with the same woman, Emilia. Arcite is released from prison, but disguises himself in order to remain close to Emilia. The jailer's daughter is in love with Palamon and helps him to escape, only to fall later into madness. A duel and a cure for the jailer's daughter ensue.

38. HENRY VIII

This last history play was written with John Fletcher, and leads up to the birth of Elizabeth I by dramatizing Henry VIII's courtship of Anne Boleyn, his separation from his first wife, the fall of his chief minister Cardinal Wolsey and their meaning for his realm. An illustration of how easily ambitious people may rise and fall.

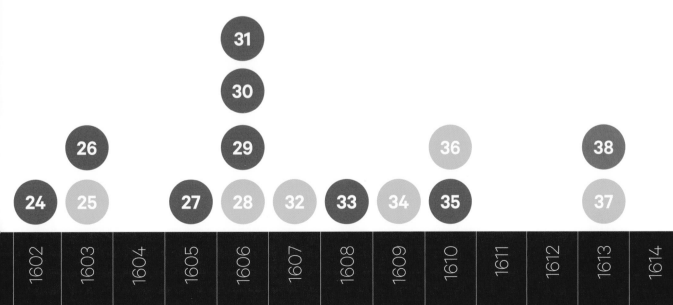

31

30

26   29   36   38

24 25   27 28 32 33 34 35   37

1602 1603 1604 1605 1606 1607 1608 1609 1610 1611 1612 1613 1614

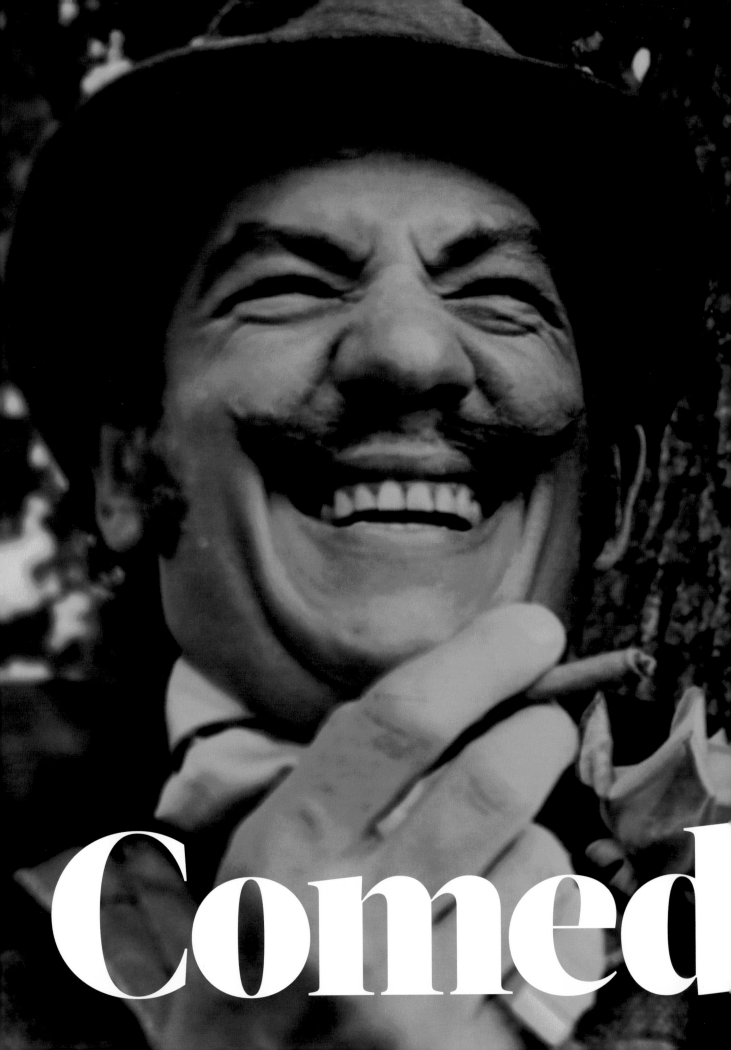

Comed

ies

ESSAYS

Love *or* money

Lucre – the possession of it, the lack of it, and how to come by it (by marrying it, for example) – is very much to the point in *The Merry Wives of Windsor*, a 'revenge comedy of jealousy' said to have been written by royal command

AUTHOR: BARBARA EVERETT

The *Merry Wives of Windsor* tells us things about Shakespeare that are not found in any other of his writings. It is always, and always has been, a riot in the theatre. But on the page, it can seem an odder work than might be expected from a happy, sane, simple little comedy. The editor of any good edition, like the Oxford or the Penguin, has serious problems to tackle. Though the text is usually listed under Comedy, its most evident affiliations are with the later Histories, some of whose most important characters it borrows: Falstaff, his hangers-on Bardolph, Pistol and Nym, Mistress Quickly, Justice Shallow. But the exact way it relates to *Henry IV, 1* and *2*, and *Henry V*, and indeed the whole question of when it was first put together, remains the subject of hot debate among scholars.

It appears that a basic plot dealing with the young couple, Fenton and Anne, derives from something written for a Garter ceremony at Windsor in 1597; and that on to this was later grafted the *Merry Wives* plot featuring the now fantastically popular and successful Sir John Falstaff. (The story of the possible occasion of this grafting, the royal command to be shown a Falstaff in love, we shall return to.) If the play was fabricated in this way, it would explain other problems.

What we have is some effect of fragmentariness. The two texts of the play, Quarto and Folio, are markedly different. There are schisms in the text: the fairy play at the end is charming in the theatre, but startling when read. Its personnel bear little resemblance to their earlier selves: Mistress Quickly (whom Falstaff seems never to have met before) steps forward transformed, speaking verse in upper-class tones. Similarly, the caricatural Frenchman, Doctor Caius, and the Welsh Parson Evans have here mislaid their accents. But the whole linguistic question is somewhat special in this comedy. It might be said that its characters are for the most part realized not by fullness of being, but by idiosyncrasy of speech: what Dr Caius really speaks is an early version of Franglais, just as Evans has contrived "Wanglais". Perhaps most eccentric is the Host of the Garter Inn, often vocal as a species of Chorus, and able with his virtuoso babble to make a reader feel that no other Shakespearean text has left behind so many unsolved cruxes. We still do not know what the Host meant by "Mockwater", and even less by "Castalian King Urinal Hector, of Greece". In fact, no one speaks full English except for Falstaff, who gets what little authority he has in the play from it.

All these verbal coruscations and cruxes are matched by *Through-the-Looking-Glass* or *Nonsense* timing. The Fairy Play salutes Shakespeare's Queen, a compliment that harmonizes with the whole pleasing illusion that Tudor Windsor has come to life before us, with its "Garter Inn", its "Castle", "Great Park", "Frogmore" and "Datchet Mead". Yet, despite all these conscientious references, the illusion is perhaps even stronger that this is Tudor Stratford. There is something snug and homey here, something redolent of a world long-known and familiar. But, if Queen Elizabeth is on the throne, then the play's young hero, Fenton, who we are carefully told kept company with Prince Hal, has to be some 200 years old, as of course does Falstaff and all the others who have stepped over from the Histories.

Elizabethans had a different sense of time from ourselves. And Shakespeare as an artist was never anything like a "realist" in the sense of "naturalist", caring for the merely factual, sociological or politico-historical. A man who likes to set a play on the sea-coast of Bohemia does not worry about a few hundred missing years. But it is not hard to see why over the past half-century or so the strongest effort among scholars has been to tidy up the play, to get it organized.

Part of the richness of *The Merry Wives* is its confusion. But I should like to explore, not what is in the play, but what isn't. Every editor will point out that *The Merry Wives* has less verse in it than any other play by Shakespeare. I would extend this into saying that the work has less poetry in it, it is simply less poetical. The canon offers many plays recognizable at sight as intensely poetic: *A Midsummer Night's Dream*

The PLOT derives from something written for a Garter CEREMONY, and a royal command to see FALSTAFF in love

BARBARA EVERETT

or *Twelfth Night* or *The Tempest, Othello* or *Macbeth* or *Antony and Cleopatra*; or plays not necessarily so plainly "beautiful" in the old-fashioned sense, but of an indestructible character that in terms of imagination achieves unity – *The Merchant of Venice, Henry IV, All's Well That Ends Well, Troilus and Cressida, Measure for Measure, Hamlet, King Lear,* or *Cymbeline*.

Henry James, in one of his lesser-known short stories, "The Special Type", defines the nature of an artist by making his painter-narrator say that "a man habitually ridden by the twin demons of imagination and observation is never – enough for his peace – out of anything". This balanced pairing of imagination and observation, the world inside the head and that outside the self, seems to me an unimprovable explanation of Shakespeare's greatness as a writer, a poet. The trouble is that our highly politicized culture has despised and abandoned imagination. It would be pointless to try to suggest, in a few paragraphs, how one of the plays listed above actually operates as a poem. Instead I want to take something as genuinely poetic in the much briefer way it works: a poem that operates as a kind of converse to, a reversal of, the delightful observation of *The Merry Wives* – Sonnet 107:

Not mine own fears, nor the prophetic soul
Of the wide world, dreaming on things to
come,
Can yet the lease of my true love control,
Supposed as forfeit to a confined doom.
The mortal moon hath her eclipse endured,
And the sad augurs mock their own presage,
Incertainties now crown themselves assured,
And peace proclaims olives of endless age.
Now with the drops of this most balmy time

My love looks fresh, and death to me
subscribes,
Since, spite of him, I'll live in this poor
rhyme,
While he insults o'er dull and speechless
tribes.
And thou in this shalt find thy monument,
When tyrants' crests and tombs of brass are
spent.

In many modern editions I know, this sonnet is given around half a dozen pages of (small-printed) annotation. It is taken to be a document packed with allusion to events contemporary with it. The key line is the fifth, "The mortal moon hath her eclipse endured". The contested explanations range from the crescent formation of the ships of the Armada in 1588 to Elizabeth's death in 1603. Though far from ridiculous, these notes do make themselves vulnerable to a charge of misreading: they don't exercise the right kind of intelligence towards language, vocabulary and syntax, tone and rhythm. If we emphasize observation so much as to ignore the imagined, we shall not know when we encounter the figurative and when the literal. In line five, the Moon is the real Moon, set on the edge of the late-medieval earthly cosmos and therefore fallen, like all our world, fated to die, "moriturus". If she is figurative at all, she is a goddess of love: pathetic because also the figure of mutability. She will one day, like us, die, and every month appears to do so – but recovers, to bear the new moon.

The "mortal" moon recovers; she dies, and endures – the process is like that tragicomic experience which is everywhere in Shakespeare's work, most articulately in his late Romances. In its triumphant embrace of and mastery over suffering in love, which has to be "endured", this sonnet's upward and soaring movement makes me read it as perhaps the first of the great happy love poems in English. The Sonnets reveal that Shakespeare could not always make himself clear, because this is thinking, not orating; private, not public; imagination, not observation: the poet is writing like Rimbaud 300 years early.

I have been hoping to define what seems essential to Shakespeare's work as a writer. The answer may be what we see revealed, both as principle and as practice, in *Sonnet 107* – the power of intelligent or "observant" imagination that works to engender at once love and poetry. The sonnet begins hauntingly from "fears", a "prophetic soul", a "wide world dreaming": *The Merry Wives* in a sense gets its very charm from its communal straightforwardness and simplicity, its lack of fears and dreams and madness and lies.

I am far from suggesting that this tolerant, good-humoured and funny play is a ferocious social satire; it is not. And yet any attentive reader may be stopped by the curiously mean and ugly lines that keep cropping up in it: as when the louse is reckoned to be "a familiar beast to man, and signifies love"; or we overhear Quickly's "we had an hour's talk of this wart", the wart identifying, for her, Anne's lover; or finally, what is surely one of Shakespeare's toughest-ever sayings about love, "They mistook their erection".

There are many more such moments in *The Merry Wives* than one might guess from accounts of the play, that seem to take us suddenly forward into the world of (say) *Troilus and Cressida*. But the "Dark" Comedies and late Romances have learned structures and styles and characters that absorb and resolve their own darknesses into a searching

tragicomedy, or (in the case of *Troilus*) a poignant, hard satire. *The Merry Wives* has not. Its harsher materials merely bump about under the surface, like Falstaff in his buck-basket.

The crooked Falstaff of *The Merry Wives* tends to provoke the whole difficult issue of whether – as the superbly sympathetic AC Bradley first complained – Falstaff is wrongly degraded in the play. The question is complex because the character is in fact not simply unitary: he has different manifestations in the *Henry IV* plays, *The Merry Wives* and *Henry V*. In *Henry IV, Part 1* he is a hero, if not in simple moral terms: he sets his intelligence, wit, vitality and imagination – his half-conscious fictions and fantasies – against the young Prince's observation of facts, his power in the real world. In *Part 2* Hal is largely absent, replaced by the surely ancient Lord Chief Justice, and indeed the whole play is peopled by the old, the ill, the bereaved. The Falstaff who swaggers in before his little page, richly dressed and diseased, preys on women and country gentlemen. He is still a formidable figure, but he is hardly any longer lovable: that will be given him back when he is dead, in *Henry V*.

Conceivably it was the use made of Falstaff in *The Merry Wives* that made Shakespeare decide not to include him (as promised) in *Henry V*. In both parts of *Henry IV* (and, posthumously, in *Henry V*) Falstaff has dignity; in *The Merry Wives*, he has little or none. He is reduced to fit in with Windsor, structured as part of a particular world. This is a character seen from the outside, and not with that aesthetic and sympathetic imagination that makes him some kind of great man in the *Henry IV* plays. *Part 1* has carefully and brilliantly cleared a space for him, in the tavern and in

BELOW
Leslie Philips
as Falstaff in
*The Merry Wives
of Windsor*
at the Royal
Shakespeare
Theatre in
Stratford-upon-Avon

play-acting, where moral values have to be called ambiguous. In drink and in play he belongs, he is inside, as he speaks to what is inside us; in *The Merry Wives*, he is an outsider to us as to the citizens who are, it has to be admitted, outsiders themselves. If our reaction here is a betrayal of the earlier fellow-feeling, then it has to be said that, along with the abandonment of love and poetry, betrayal is itself predominant in the comedy.

Merry the wives certainly are, even in the gusto with which they congratulate themselves and each other on having their revenge on both Falstaff and Ford. Without doubt the men are not pleasing, as Ford says to Falstaff, "Want no money, Sir John; you shall want none", and the old man answers, "Want no Mistress Ford, Master Brook; you shall want none". There is a sinister shadow here almost on a level with the early exchanges between Roderigo and Iago in *Othello*. And indeed *The Merry Wives* is a revenge comedy of jealousy.

How did so much revenge get into the play? In ordinary life, a woman subject to passes she doesn't want may think less of the intelligence of the maker of the pass, or she may smile formally and gratefully and pass on her way: revenge is surely unlikely to be in question. But there is in this comedy a mechanism of preconception, which gives it its farcical speed and smartness, and its crispness of intrigue in action; and if the wives are angry, it is probably Falstaff's inability to distinguish between them, with his sign-on-the-line love letters, that gets their goat.

The strength of this play is the deep interconnections Shakespeare sees, even as necessities, between money, jealousy and revenge. The testimony of the plays in general is that where love is powered by imagination, we feel sympathy: and only then are unable to use others, to see them as wealth or possessions. If love entails such ownership it breeds jealousy.

The trouncing of Falstaff by the wives is often wildly funny on stage: we at once want him to be taught a lesson by his intended prey, but also saved from his manic hunter, Ford, and this double laughter of triumph and relief gives the great scene of the laundry-basket its delight. Yet even here there are curiously dark shadows. The basket is always referred to as what it is, a buck-basket: this meant the container carrying dirty household linen away to be bleached, before washing, by being steeped in lye, that is to say human urine – a classic method, at least as old as Rome. The buck-basket says this, but not poetically. Falstaff is next unsexed by being smuggled out as a fat, bearded and finally beaten-up old woman, with witchy attributes. He is last horned as both hunter and hunted, and presumably too as "cornuto", cuckold, betrayed lover of neither woman, pinched by fairies in the moonlight before being, like Parolles in *All's Well*, graciously accepted by his former tormentors. Windsor and Stratford have done their best against the dangerous principles of love and art.

There are conclusions to be drawn by considering the lack, in *The Merry Wives*, of poetry, of Shakespearean thinking and the working methods that are found elsewhere in his work. Anecdotes by John Dennis and Nicholas Rowe declare the play to have originated in royal command, and to have been written in a very few weeks. This kind of productivity is the reverse of what might be taken to be the poet's essential working method, as evidenced in both substance and style by *Sonnet 107*. This is the procedure philosophers call "emergence", or living evolution: by which, in Browning's rhetoric, three sounds come to make not a fourth sound, but a star. It is reasonable to conjecture that the poet's subconscious was always in process of gathering, hoarding, and making slow use of what it stored, not unlike the way Wordsworth spoke of himself as using materials from "hiding-places ten years deep". What many scholars assume now to be evidence of revision or collaboration may merely be a case of the writer drawing forward ideas, instances and phrases from different experiences, different times and occasions: what Dryden described in a fine phrase as a writer's "moving the sleeping images of things towards the light". It occurs everywhere in Shakespeare's work, and underlies the impossibility of paraphrasing *Sonnet 107*. *The Merry Wives* is by comparison mechanical.

And to see this is perhaps to justify the story told about the Queen's command. Such a commission was unignorable, but left no time for "sleeping images", for idiosyncratic work powered from within. And Shakespeare did it marvellously well. One of Falstaff's mellow pieces of wit in it is his "Let it thunder to the tune of *Greensleeves*", and this is close to the effect of the whole.

It is hard to believe that Shakespeare, severely pushed for time, and making use of everything conceivably within his reach, did not build his country world out of twenty-five years of memories in his own head. If this is Tudor Stratford, Shakespeare's birthplace had real virtues of tough good sense, equable balance of mind and a rare eye for the main chance. I earlier quoted from Henry James's "The Special Type", but another equally little-known tale is useful here. "The Papers" tells how two lower-middle-class, idealistic and talented but struggling young journalists, friends and finally in love, never for a moment think of leaving London and trying elsewhere, because "the town, if it did nothing else, gave a range to the spirit". The novelist of course means a metaphor here, but perhaps he is also held by a touching sense of the literal: of the tremendous walks around the great city indulged in for centuries – back through Henry James himself to Samuel Johnson, and from Johnson, perhaps, to the young William Shakespeare – by those brilliantly open to life and experience but lacking the means to afford any other pleasures. It is that "range to the spirit" that Shakespeare had to go to London to find. In *The Merry Wives*' smallness, cosiness, snugness and slight mindlessness we miss that range. But the play is unique, and it is a revelation to encounter a great artist in reverse, and see what he can do when forced to use little but his genius for hard work. ∎

When LOVE is powered by imagination, when it doesn't see people as wealth or possessions, we feel SYMPATHY

BARBARA EVERETT

Viola, disguised as a boy, is dispatched by her lord Orsino to woo Olivia for him; but Olivia is more taken with the messenger than the master.

"Make me willow your gat call upon within th

OLIVIA Your lord does know my mind: I cannot love him.
Yet I suppose him virtuous, know him noble,
Of great estate, of fresh and stainless youth;
In voices well divulged, free, learned and valiant,
And in dimension and the shape of nature
A gracious person; but yet I cannot love him.
He might have took his answer long ago.
VIOLA If I did love you in my master's flame,
With such a suff'ring, such a deadly life,
In your denial I would find no sense,
 I would not understand it.

OLIVIA Why, what would you?
VIOLA Make me a willow cabin at your gate,
And call upon my soul within the house,
Write loyal cantons of contemnèd love
And sing them loud even in the dead of night,
Hallow your name to the reverberate hills
And make the babbling gossip of the air
Cry out "Olivia!" O, you should not rest
Between the elements of air and earth,
But you should pity me!
OLIVIA You might do much.

a cabin at e, And my soul e house"

Twelfth Night, act 1 scene 5

Fairy dust

A Midsummer Night's Dream

Rose Theatre, Kingston, 2010

Judi Dench reunited with Peter Hall to play Titania 48 years after she first tackled the role for the director. Time had withered neither her performance, nor Hall's sure eye

AUTHOR: JULIET FLEMING

Could it be that *A Midsummer Night's Dream* is not a very good play? It has three scarcely related actions – the bumpy course of young love, the difficulty (especially if you are an ignorant bumpkin) of staging a play, and a climate-changing stand-off between the King and Queen of the fairies. Its characters are walking contradictions.

Titania falls in love with an ass-headed plebeian without finally compromising her dignity, Theseus is a bland tyrant, and his bride a docile warrior, the two heroines Hermia and Helena engage in a cat fight designed to humiliate them (the 1999 film version of the play staged this scene, with some justification, as mud-wrestling), the male lovers are fickle and quarrelsome, and Oberon is at once menacing, petty and committed to helping human love run smooth. Beyond this, the language of the play doesn't always fit the occasion: for example, Oberon's famously beautiful lines, beginning "I know a bank whereon the wild thyme grows", elaborate his scheme to

pluck a flower whose properties will allow him to humiliate the Fairy Queen, and force her to release to his care the child she loves.

It can be argued that such dramatic inconsistencies are essentially English (perhaps as the expression of an island pragmatism that can't be bothered to get things quite right). Alternatively, they can be held to demonstrate the genius of a playwright who – as Peter Hall puts it in the programme notes for his production at the Rose – "while looking honestly at the absurdity of human behaviour, ends up celebrating it". Shakespeare's lack of judgement in such matters has long been admired, and Ben Jonson's caveat, that Shakespeare should not be admired for never having crossed out a line ("I had rather", Jonson says, "he had blotted

a thousand"), is dismissed as the criticism of a rival poet who put correctness before greatness.

A Midsummer Night's Dream, in particular, celebrates the power of theatre to move audiences in ways for which there is no accounting. As if by way of pre-empting criticism, Bottom describes the action in famous terms: "I have had a dream. It would pass the wit of man to say what dream it was: man is but an ass, if he go about to expound this dream". Still, however we excuse, explain or admire them, we might acknowledge that most of Shakespeare's plays contain elements that pose considerable challenges – as well as local opportunities – to the actors and directors who undertake them.

Peter Hall's latest production, staged on a spare and pretty set at

ABOVE
Judi Dench as Titania hugs Paul Rogers's Bottom in Peter Hall's 1968 film adaptation of *A Midsummer Night's Dream*

the jewel-like Rose Theatre, Kingston (where Hall, now eighty, is the emeritus director), makes the most of these opportunities. In 1962, when the world was young, Hall directed the play as the founder and artistic director of the Royal Shakespeare Company at Stratford. In 1968 the production was made into a film (scenes from which can

A great actor ACTING both her part, and herself in her part – a remarkable MOMENT of British theatre history

JULIET FLEMING

now be watched on YouTube) starring, among others, Diana Rigg as Helena, Helen Mirren as Hermia and Judi Dench as a staggeringly compelling Titania.

The genius of casting Dench in the same role forty-eight years later is evident: nothing in the play suggests that the Queen of the Fairies should be young; indeed her practised resistance to her husband Oberon perhaps suggests otherwise. Hall dresses Dench as Elizabeth I, and stages the play as if it were a production at court in which the Queen has agreed to take a leading part, but the justification is not necessary.

The ease with which Dench takes up the role, her mastery of Shakespeare's verse line, and the tenderness that emerges between herself and Bottom (the hugely talented Oliver Chris) more than justify Hall's having chosen her for the role (or, more likely, having chosen the play for her). Dench says she has never seen the film in which she starred, but her current performance, which seems closely modelled on that earlier one, puts audiences in the presence of a great actor acting both her part, and herself in her part, and so makes for a remarkable moment of British theatre history. All the same, there is something aloof about this Fairy Queen. As Queen Elizabeth, Dench does not compromise her dignity by engaging with her courtiers as she silently agrees to take a part in their play; and as Titania she is not impressed by Oberon, and has very little interest in her fairy entourage.

Perhaps an actor of the age, stature and experience of Judi Dench must anyway look with some detachment on those who still have a lot to learn.

With the exception of Reece Ritchie, who recites Puck's short lines with the bumbling irony of a schoolboy forced onstage, every member of the cast can make speaking sense of Shakespeare's verse. But few of them can find the emotional centre of the parts they have been allotted: Oberon (Charles Edwards) is furious about something, he doesn't quite know what; Demetrius (Ben Mansfield) concentrates on pronouncing his lines rather than using them to any sensible effect; Lysander (Tam Williams) has a random intensity and no place to put it; and Theseus (Julian Wadham) speaks into the far distance rather than to anyone else, blandly delivering his surprising and inconsistent

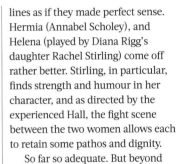

BELOW
Judi Dench with
Ian Richardson, who
plays the Fairy King,
Oberon, in the film
of *A Midsummer
Night's Dream*

lines as if they made perfect sense. Hermia (Annabel Scholey), and Helena (played by Diana Rigg's daughter Rachel Stirling) come off rather better. Stirling, in particular, finds strength and humour in her character, and as directed by the experienced Hall, the fight scene between the two women allows each to retain some pathos and dignity.

So far so adequate. But beyond the presence of Dench, a second reason to see this production is the *tour de force* of Oliver Chris as Bottom, supported by his fellow Mechanicals. All the costumes in this production are intelligent, and many of them gorgeous, but the ass's head is something to marvel at: when Chris has it on he moves like a well-proportioned animal, and looks not monstrous under Dench's be-ringed hands, but strangely attractive: the delight the two actors take in pulling off this coup is both evident and infectious. But Chris is equally good before and after his transformation. James Laurenson (Quince), Leon Williams (Flute), Timothy Speyer (Snug), Simon Scott (Snout) and William Chubb (Starveling) are flawless as the workmen who, with Bottom, rehearse and stage the play of *Pyramus and Thisbe*; and they provide a secure space within which Chris can both find the pathos in Bottom's character, and liberate its enormous comic potential. As the dying Pyramus, Chris holds the audience's delighted attention longer than the writing warrants, and then – just because he can – holds it some more. And here his achievement – as the actor acting to move us because he can – rivals that of Dench. ■

ESSAYS

A toast of Bohemia

The Czechs' love affair with Shakespeare began long before the 'Velvet Revolution'. His plays have a long, honorable history of translation and adaptation as commentaries on the challenges of life behind the Iron Curtain

AUTHOR: LOIS POTTER

A large red neon heart on Prague Castle commemorated Václav Havel's presidency, now officially ended. Apparently, he has sometimes used the heart as part of his signature. I imagine educated Prague opinion found the heart on the castle a little vulgar. But, "I think it is all right – for a little while", said Zdeněk Stříbrný, the retired professor of English and American studies at Charles University. Zdeněk can put up with almost anything, so long as he knows it won't last, and, in his experience, very little does.

I was in Prague to work with Zdeněk on an autobiographical introduction to a collection of his essays that my university press hopes to publish. This is the third time I have been there for this purpose: Zdeněk, who is now on his second pacemaker, has been told to take things easy and drink red wine, so the process is going slowly. Neither of us minds. I spend the mornings reading and commenting on Zdeněk's life, the life of someone for whom 1968 meant transfer from the School of English and American Studies to the School of Mathematics and the removal of his publications from the library at Charles University. In the afternoon or evening we go

ABOVE
Václav Havel, playwright, essayist dissident and the president of the Czech Republic from 1993 to 2003

into town and see a Shakespeare play. Mindful of its need to attract tourists, Prague offers a good deal of entertainment that needs no knowledge of Czech: the Magic Lantern Theatre, pantomime, concerts by candlelight with performers in period costume, opera (especially *Don Giovanni*), and touring productions in other languages. But Czech Shakespeare

isn't aimed at tourists, though some theatres now offer a programme in English. The plays have a long history of translation and adaptation as commentaries on contemporary life. This function was particularly important before 1989, when contemporary plays – not just political plays but absurdist drama, which was considered too elitist – found it hard to get a hearing. When spectators went to see the classic repertory, they did so in order to join with the actors in a collective act of misreading, usually directed at the Russian occupation forces.

My first non-tourist visit came about six months after the "Velvet Revolution". Everyone kept saying that theatre attendances were down because people were now able to watch more exciting events on their television screens, but simply looking at the cast list was meaningful for those, like Zdeněk, who knew which of the actors had been unable to perform in Prague during the previous regime.

The first thing I saw in post-revolutionary Prague was a British touring company performing Havel's three Vaněk plays in English translation. It was the first time for more than ten years that a Prague

The nineteenth-century
National Theatre in
Prague, which stages
drama, ballet and opera

audience had been able to see the work of their future president. In those days very few Czechs knew English, but the theatre was crowded anyway. As we entered, we saw that most of the audience was queuing up for headsets so as to listen to a simultaneous translation back into the original Czech. The actor playing Vaněk was made up to look like Havel. The experience was midway between art and life, which is how they like it in Prague.

Nowadays, everyone in the vast Czech tourist industry speaks some English, but in pre-revolutionary Prague the small number of fluent English-speakers belonged to a special world. University professors not only taught but also translated the literature of the languages they knew best. Members of the translators' union were designated as guides to visiting literary celebrities.

There were disadvantages to being so visible: one professor of English told me about receiving an invitation to a British Council reception and, almost simultaneously, a telephone call from the Russian head of the foreign languages department, ordering him to come over immediately and to bring the invitation.

In the Writers' and Translators' Club, a comfortable place which is now a casualty of the revolution (the property turned out to have been confiscated long ago from a dentist who wanted it back), I talked to Břetislav Hodek, Christopher Fry's official translator. He told me that he nearly got into trouble over his neat solution to a pun in *The Lady's Not for Burning*. "Tedium, tedium, tedium", the first line of Act Three, seems, at least since Gielgud first played Thomas Mendip, to have merged into "Tiddy-um, tiddy-um, tiddy-um".

The translator had dealt with this one by moving from "nuda", which is "boredom" in Czech, to "Nu, da", the Russian for "Well, yes". Merely the sound of Russian was enough to get a laugh, as with Spanish in Italian Renaissance comedies.

Martin Hilský, who translated *Love's Labour's Lost* for a National Theatre production, has written of the effect in performance of an episode that looks totally innocuous on the page: the King of Navarre and his courtiers, costumed as Russians, tell the Princess and her ladies that they want "nothing but peace and gentle visitation" and the Princess replies that they have it and therefore should "be gone". The disguised courtiers in this version spoke real Russian and no one could miss the coincidence between their wishes and "Mir y druzhba", or the Princess's expression of the sentiments of the whole population.

After the revolution, this kind of collective decoding became harder to achieve because the key to the code – a unanimous audience attitude – no longer existed. Shakespeare goes on being produced, however: as the author most frequently seen on the stage, he has become a site of comparison and competition for both translators and directors, and to that extent reflects the new era. *The Winter's Tale* is a favourite play in the country because of the Bohemian scenes, which in the era of realistic staging sometimes located King Polixenes in Prague Castle. Every Czech who knows the play must always watch for the moment in which voyagers arrive on the coast of this notoriously landlocked country. When I saw it, Hilský's translation of the line, "Thou art perfect, then, our ship hath touched

GETTY

ABOVE
Havel became a focus for popular protest in Czechoslovakia

upon the deserts of Bohemia?" was spoken in disbelieving tones – something like "Are you sure the ship has landed on the deserts of Bohemia?" Without knowing the exact words, I understood it perfectly. Watching Shakespeare in Czech, I realized, was probably what watching Shakespeare in English must be like for many of my students. One is really going on tone of voice and gesture for much of the time; though, given the strongly physical and visual nature of theatre in Central Europe, this isn't too difficult.

In this winter of 2003, full of forebodings of war, the two plays for which Zdeněk had tickets were *The Comedy of Errors* and *Romeo and Juliet*. They were performed in the most beautiful acting spaces in the city: the gold-and-silver-gilt National Theatre and the Estates Theatre (where *Don Giovanni* had its premiere), both restored to a degree of glitter I have never seen in England or America. Its low-comedy, improvised quality allowed *The Comedy of Errors* (directed by the Hungarian Enikő Eszenyi) to be the more political of the two. Probably no director could resist adding to the scene in which the Syracusan Antipholus encourages Dromio to compare the various parts of a fat kitchen maid to the geographical locations best known to Shakespeare ("Where stood… the Netherlands?" "O, sir, I did not look so low"). Inevitably, this Antipholus also asked "Where is the Czech Republic?"

Zdeněk, who is getting rather hard of hearing, couldn't tell me exactly what the answer was, or why everyone was laughing, but I guessed that Dromio was saying, "It doesn't know where it is until it gets into the EEC".

The rest of the production felt equally topical, though even Zdeněk couldn't explain exactly how. Ephesus, the play's setting, was a totalitarian state, and in the opening scene Duke Solinus interrogated an obviously roughed-up Egeon. The old man's story was accompanied by the playing of confiscated CDs from his briefcase – home videos, from years ago, of the two sets of twin children running around a big sheltering tree. As the images sputtered to an end, Egeon reached longingly towards the screen in an effort to clasp, not the children,

ROMEO and JULIET – Czechs relate to the theme of HAPPINESS thwarted by the wars of a previous generation

LOIS POTTER

but the tree. The action then moved to central Ephesus, with a revolving set representing a sleazy part of Prague, including nightclub, dress shop, and the apartment building of the Ephesian Antipholus.

Warned against revealing their true nationality, the Syracusan Antipholus and Dromio had their photos taken by an underground operator who supplied them with false ID cards. Mafiosi prowled the streets. The address of the Ephesian Antipholus – 68 Jarní Street – was conspicuous not only on the building but also on the dustbin out front. Zdeněk pointed out to me that Jarní means "spring", and that the dustbin therefore held the Prague Spring of 1968. This visual pun was clearly a key to the director's reading of Ephesus as a disillusioned and loveless culture, capable of nothing but farce. But the reunion of Egeon's family took place under the same tree we had seen on video, now bathed in spring sunshine.

Romeo and Juliet is a favourite play in Prague, because everyone can relate to the theme of human happiness thwarted by the wars of a previous generation. I had already seen an energetic and youthful version in a small theatre where the actors literally climbed the walls of the set, as well as a splendidly imaginative production of Gounod's opera. Making the Capulets and Montagues into West and East Berliners might seem rather obvious, but the director generalized from this political conflict by using ballet dancers as the warring forces of love and death (in white tutus and black leather respectively).

Sometimes the dancers took over the physical action while the singers expressed abstract emotion; against the harshness of the setting, Gounod's music wasn't a lush anachronism

but an agonized outpouring of desire for something different.

Vladimír Morávek's new production of the play used a translation by Josef Topol from the 1960s, the period leading up to the Prague Spring. (Since Zdeněk edited a complete edition of Shakespeare in Czech translation, he always notices such choices, which are never innocent.) Whereas most Czech productions use modern dress, this one dressed the characters in Italian Renaissance costume. In the opening moments, a row of masked men in black confronted another row of masked women in white. Zdeněk whispered that we were already at the ball and that Mercutio was speaking the Queen Mab speech. After the exchange in which Mercutio agrees with Romeo that he is only talking of dreams, three women in black peasant costumes – the three fates? – entered and spoke the prologue antiphonally. Each was carrying a long-stemmed red rose, which she threw into the ground like a dart; roses recurred throughout the play, finally visible as a mass of colour below Juliet's tomb. The women remained on stage to speak the stage directions for characters' first entrances; they also re-entered to speak the act and scene numbers. There was no pretence that we were hearing the story for the first time; the actors were there just to remind us of it, sometimes in a rather abbreviated rendering of the text. This didn't prevent the production from being moving, especially in the final scene, where the Capulets and the Montagues take hands. As with *The Comedy of Errors*, the reconciliation was staged as too good to be true. If perfect love is a dream, the idea that tragedy can lead to the reconciliation of enemies is even more of one. The red roses reminded me of the red heart on Prague Castle, which of course has now been removed. ∎

Comedies

Mostly written early in his career, Shakespeare's comedies – with their multiple, interweaving plots, robust humour, mistaken identities and star-crossed lovers – are powered by social and political satire

"In Shakespeare's high comedy the tradition and technique of classical comedy, with its intrigues and its satiric condemnation of all aberration from a materialistic social norm, is transformed into something new and lovely, at once the promise and perfection of a more abundant life – into a comedy that expands, not contracts, the heart."
JOHN MIDDLETON MURRY, 1938

"As Stephen Orgel says, 'Shakespeare loves loose ends'. Does Isabella accept the Duke's proposal in *Measure for Measure*? Will Malvolio release the sea-captain, so allowing Viola to recover her woman's weeds? Will the chaps in *Love's Labour's Lost* be rewarded with the ladies, once they have completed their year's community service? The answer to the last of these questions would probably have been found in the sequel, *Love's Labour's Won*, the most tantalizing of Shakespeare's lost works... "
JONATHAN BATE, 2000

"Shakespeare's tragedies do not, by and large, end problematically. Death really is an ending, audiences tend to believe in it, and after the excesses of *Titus Andronicus*, Shakespeare became a better dramatist than those of his contemporaries who nowadays reduce an audience to giggles as they pile up the corpses stage centre. The conventions of tragedy present fewer problems to the truthful dramatist than the conventions of the patriotic epic, or those of romantic comedy. Our own cynicism about

marriage apart, it is undeniable that it is much harder to end a play convincingly with a wedding than it is with a funeral. The comedic formula requires multiple marriages; the Shakespearean truth as often as not points in the other direction. The result is that audiences sometimes part company with a play, or laugh at it. I have seen *Twelfth Night* a lot, and directed it recently at the Lincoln Center in New York. If there has been a performance where the audience has been convinced by Orsino's proposal of marriage to Viola, I can't remember it. Generally, they react with contempt."
NICHOLAS HYTNER, 2002

"Because both its romantic and its dark sides are extravagant, and inconsistent in action, tone and morality, *The Two Gentlemen of Verona* has had fewer professional productions than many other Shakespearean comedies. It has, however, long been a favourite with amateurs, especially when playing outdoors, where what jangles in the text can be attributed to the actors or discounted in the garden context of the occasion... The apprentice playwright's large ambitions are already clear in the early work, for the nexus of the strife between love and friendship had been discussed by philosophers and dramatized by poets for centuries. Beyond bravura technical mastery, what changed in his writing included a shift to women whose unironic constancy finally redeems the unreliable, and sometimes tawdry, objects of their affections."
RUTH MORSE, 2008

Prospero

Iain Crichton Smith

When I left that island I thought I was dead.
Nothing stirred in me. Miranda in jeans
and totally innocent was standing by a sail
and all the others, happily recovered, talking
in suits made of brine. But to return to

the gossip, the poisonous ring, was not easy,
and many times I nearly tried to turn back
feeling in my bones the desolate hum of the headland,
my creation of rivers and mist.

Still we went on. The corruptible had put on flesh,
the young were hopeful once again, all was forgiven.
Nevertheless the waiters were scraping and bowing.
the rumours beginning, the crowns of pure crystal were sparkling
the telephones were ringing with messages from the grave
and the thin phosphorescent boys glowing with ambition
in corners of velvet and death.

Still I went on. The ship left its wake behind it
shining and fading, cord of a new birth,
and over by the sail Miranda gazed at her prince
yearning for love.

Goodbye, island, never again shall I see you,
you are part of my past. Though I may dream of you often
I know there's a future we all must learn to accept
music working itself out in the absurd halls and the mirrors
posturing of men like birds, Art in a torrent of plates,
the sound of the North wind distant yet close
as stairs ascend from the sea.

ILLUSTRATION: VALENTINA VERC

*At the end of The Tempest,
Prospero and his daughter Miranda
leave their enchanted island; this
poem imagines what happens next.*

Histori

es

ESSAYS

A bard's eye-view

The late sixteenth and early seventeenth centuries were a period
of great Welsh cultural influence on England. Shakespeare included
Welsh characters in all of the English history plays except *King John*

AUTHOR: DAVID HAWKES

Did it seem like a fine idea at the time? On November 24, 2007, in Cardiff's Millennium Stadium, the Welsh national rugby team battled South Africa for the inaugural Prince William Cup. It was natural enough that the Prince should present the cup in person. After the visitors' victory, William's smiling face filled the stadium big screen. But as the Prince brandished the prize, his smile suddenly flickered. His eyes darted. An unaccustomed noise filled his ears. Could it be? Surely not! And yet it was. To the BBC commentators' baffled annoyance, to William's visible consternation, but to the surprise of nobody at all in his Principality, there rang from the stands the unmistakable sound of prolonged and sincere booing.

What was going on? Everybody in Wales knew. A few months earlier, Welsh fans had been angered by the sight of the Prince wearing the national rugby shirt of England. Few English people could understand this anger: certainly, it seemed incomprehensible to the Prince. Wasn't he simply displaying a natural patriotic pride in his country? But to Welsh eyes it looked like an aggressive act. The Prince was announcing his allegiance to a polity that emphatically excluded them. It was an untimely reminder that the future Prince of Wales was, like all his predecessors since the thirteenth century, an Englishman.

There had certainly been Welsh claimants to the title. Before the game against South Africa the mischievous Welsh stadium announcer appealed to the crowd to honour the recently deceased Llanelli centre Ray Gravell as "gwir Dywysog Cymru" the "true Prince of Wales". A petition was launched, backed by several Welsh MPs, to rename the Prince William trophy after Gravell. Some even suggested that the most appropriate sobriquet would be the Glyn Dwr Cup, after the last Welshman to aspire to be Prince of his nation. It was an idea of which Shakespeare would have heartily approved.

Although English literary historians have barely acknowledged the fact, the

BELOW
The Welsh rugby
team lost the Prince
William Cup to South
Africa in 2007. The
royal who gave the
cup its name was
booed as he passed
it to the victors

late sixteenth and early seventeenth centuries were a period of massive Welsh cultural influence on England. Apart from the Tudors themselves, many other prominent families of the day had Welsh roots, the Cecils (originally Sitsyllt) and the Cromwells among them. Queen Elizabeth's court magus, John Dee, was of Welsh ancestry, as were the major Metaphysical poets. The strenuous, strained language of Metaphysical verse is English as written by outsiders. George Herbert, Henry Vaughan and Thomas Traherne were Welsh by birth, as was the father of John Donne (originally Dwn). Donne's Welsh connections are especially suggestive, since he could claim descent from the greatest Welsh hero of all, Owain Glyn Dwr himself.

Shakespeare's Princes of Wales: English Identity and the Welsh Connection, Marisa Cull's absorbing and innovative book, demonstrates the profound significance of Wales in general, and Glyn Dwr in particular, for the life and work of Shakespeare.

The Bard (the very term has a specifically Welsh provenance) had a Welsh grandmother, Alys Griffin. The man who taught him his "small Latin", the Stratford grammar school teacher Thomas Jenkins, was Welsh. At least four of Shakespeare's colleagues in the Lord Chamberlain's men were from Wales. Welsh characters feature in all the English history plays except *King John*, as well as in *The Merry Wives of Windsor*. *Cymbeline* and *King Lear* are set in Celtic Britain, at a time before the English bestowed their current, paradoxical appellation on the Welsh. Even the historical Macbeth had Welsh connections.

As Shakespeare was well aware, Wales is England's original Other. The Saxon word *Welsch* means "foreigner". The verb *elschen*, to speak gibberish, literally means to speak like a Welshman. The history of English colonialism begins with war on the Welsh, and the colonial dichotomy between centre and periphery has its original in the fraught relations between England and Wales. The contradictory nature of this relation is encapsulated in the very title "Prince of Wales". The Principality is assigned a permanently junior, aspirant role, which can never issue in promotion or fulfilment. Welsh identity is sublimated within the English power structure, Welsh history is assimilated into an

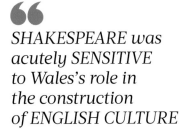

> *SHAKESPEARE was acutely SENSITIVE to Wales's role in the construction of ENGLISH CULTURE*

DAVID HAWKES

English narrative, and Welsh people are represented by an Englishman.

It is in the nature of such disproportionate relations that the dominant partner is unaware of the subordinate's real nature, identity and even existence until forcibly reminded of them, as Prince William discovered. Yet Shakespeare, greatest of all English literary heroes, was acutely sensitive to Wales's fundamental role in the construction of English national culture and character. As Cull demonstrates, he embodied and explored the resulting ambiguities through the indisputably central, yet simultaneously marginal, figure of the Prince of Wales.

This book's title is arrestingly plural. As Cull notes, most readers of Shakespeare identify his Prince of Wales with a single figure: Prince Hal. Even in the plays that he dominates, however, Hal is never the only character associated with that title. Glendower disputes it vigorously, of course, but so does Mortimer, who claimed it as the rightful heir of Richard II. The Henriad features not one but three princes of Wales, each of whom has a very different conception of the role and its functions. *Cymbeline*'s Guiderius is also Prince of Wales (Cull links these characters to the princes of Wales who feature in the period's non-Shakespearean drama, such as *The Valiant Welshman*, and Ben Jonson's *For the Honor of Wales*).

The Prince of Wales, in short, seems to have provided early modern English culture with a kind of symbolic cipher, a floating signifier, on which a vast range of aspirations and anxieties could be projected. As Cull puts it, the role was "part sovereign, part symbol". This ambiguity was facilitated by the eloquent absence of any real Prince of Wales. Henry VII's promising son Prince Arthur died prematurely

in 1502, and the famously infertile Tudors did not produce a replacement. It was not until 1610 that, following an acrimonious and undignified dispute with his reluctant father, Prince Henry Frederick was invested with the title, only to pass away himself two years later.

In the meantime, the conveniently vacant position provided playwrights with a royal personage through whom unofficial political and ideological theories could be vented without fear of offending any actual occupant. The title is not inherited automatically but bestowed in a formal ceremony of investiture, and this opened a space for its nature to be disputed. The figurehead of the Jacobean Protestants, Prince Henry Frederick, agitated to be invested without delay; his cautious father thwarted his ambition for years in an effort to preserve the delicate Elizabethan settlement. The works of Shakespeare, and other writers who dealt with Welsh themes, offered oblique but lucid commentary on this quarrel.

In *Henry IV, Part 1*, Prince Hal is called "the Prince of Wales" fourteen times. For Cull this amounts to a "fetishization" of the title, and it concentrates the audience's attention firmly on the Principality's significance and implications. It provides a way of domesticating the disturbingly "wild Welsh" who are memorably represented by the sinister women mutilating the English dead after Glendower's crushing victory at Bryn Glas. This "beastly shameless transformation", in which the Englishmen's penises are pushed into their mouths and their noses inserted into their anuses, stands for the unnatural inversion of order implied by a Welsh victory over England. That sort of thing is not supposed to happen outside rugby stadiums.

It happens in Shakespeare, though, and more than once. This was partly due to the necessity of understanding pre-Saxon British history as the ancestor of the Tudor–Stuart state. It was a tricky operation. The exploits of Arthur and Merlin were part of the island's heroic heritage, and its sixteenth- and seventeenth-century rulers were anxious to claim them as their own. The problem was that the deeds of the ancient Britons did not involve the ancestors of the English. On the contrary, they were performed in the doughty but doomed struggle against them. To acknowledge this, however, would have opened wounds that were by no means entirely healed. Some way had to be found of reading the Welsh as admirable forebears, rather than as defeated natives.

That is where Shakespeare came in. When Fluellen rams a leek down Pistol's mocking throat in *Henry V*, the hideous inversion perpetrated by the women of Bryn Glas is domesticated into a comic incident quite compatible with allegiance to the English king. When Henry V declares "I am Welsh, you know", despite his total lack of Celtic blood, the Other becomes part of the Self. When Richard III refers to Henry Tudor as "the Welshman", the coming dynasty is heralded as incorporating an originally hostile resistance into the colonial power. By such means, Shakespeare continues the project of unification inaugurated by the historical Henry when he named his son Arthur, began his victorious campaign for the throne at Milford Haven, and marched to Bosworth under the standard of the red dragon.

This domesticating project's success is described with a typically Shakespearean ambiguity. Glendower

is an outlandish figure, often played for laughs on the English stage. But his monolingual daughter brings the Welsh language onto that stage, and her marriage to Mortimer places it in a central position. Cull offers some speculation as to how widely understood such speeches might have been in London, where the Welsh would have been a highly visible minority. The language would have been at once familiar and mysterious to English people, as Hotspur suggests when he tells Glendower: "Let me not understand you, then; speak it in Welsh".

With contrary Welsh oppugnancy, Glendower refuses to obey, instead taking the chance to remind Hotspur that "I can speak English, lord, as well as you; / For I was train'd up in the English court". This training seems to have been ineffectual: Glendower is possibly the least English of all Shakespeare's characters. The play makes a game attempt to defang him. Shakespeare even informs us that he is "certainly" dead, eliding the mysterious fate of the historical Glyn Dwr, who seems to have vanished into the Monmouth mist like the phantom to which he was often compared. Nobody knows what happened to him, thought it seems likely that he found a final redoubt in the home of his daughter, Alys.

What's in a name? We cannot know how much influence Alys Griffin had over her grandson, William Shakespeare, though early twentieth-century critics like Frederick Harries enjoyed speculating that "the Celtic strain in Shakespeare's blood may be held to account for the sporadic appearance of genius in an unremarkable middle-class family". But it is clear that, despite Glendower's reported demise, Shakespeare depicted the Welsh

RIGHT
Richard Burton as Prince Hal in 1951 at the Shakespeare Memorial Theatre, Stratford-upon-Avon

with a vaguely querulous foreboding, especially where the English monarchy was concerned. The Prince of Wales is, after all, the rightful heir to the English throne, and all rulers must be slightly nervous about their heirs. In *Richard II*, it is the Welsh captain whose astrological hermeneutics leads him to declare: "These signs forerun the death or fall of kings".

Cull's essential argument is that, in Shakespeare's treatments, "the Welsh become predictors of the king's fate". The Prince of Wales is a living embodiment of that prediction. By definition he occupies an awkward, transitional position, always awaiting his parent's demise, which must take place before he can grasp his own proper destiny. It is a position of inadequacy, of unfulfilment, as the current holder of the title suggested when he lamented that "I feel I must justify my existence". Certainly, Shakespeare's English monarchs are well aware of the subversive potential inherent in the Princedom. Just after his coronation, Henry IV shows his prescience when he anxiously inquires after Hal, remarking: "If any plague hang over us, 'tis he".

The Saxon colonization of Celtic Britain provides the earliest, paradigmatic instance of English imperialism's skill at conscripting those it has conquered into its service. But as Prince William of Wales discovered in Cardiff, the colonized Other is always waiting for an opportunity, no matter how slight it may appear, to assert its continued existence, often to the dominant power's dismay and confusion. As Hal informs Douglas: "It is the Prince of Wales that threatens thee, / Who never promiseth but he means to pay". But who is the Prince of Wales? ∎

Before the Battle of Agincourt, against superior numbers, the king rallies his men.

"For he to
that sh
his
with me
be my

"**day**
eds
blood
Shall
brother "

Henry V, act 4, scene 3

HENRY V Old men forget: yet all shall be forgot,
But he'll remember with advantages
What feats he did that day: then shall our names.
Familiar in his mouth as household words
Harry the king, Bedford and Exeter,
Warwick and Talbot, Salisbury and Gloucester,
Be in their flowing cups freshly remember'd.
This story shall the good man teach his son;
And Crispin Crispian shall ne'er go by,
From this day to the ending of the world,
But we in it shall be remember'd;
We few, we happy few, we band of brothers;
For he to-day that sheds his blood with me
Shall be my brother; be he ne'er so vile,
This day shall gentle his condition:
And gentlemen in England now a-bed
Shall think themselves accursed they were not here,
And hold their manhoods cheap whiles any speaks
That fought with us upon Saint Crispin's day.

REVIEWS

Genuinely fake

Henry IV, Parts One and Two

Olivier Theatre, London, 2005

As Prince Hal and his disreputable ally Falstaff, Matthew Macfadyen and Michael Gambon gave a crash-course on courtly politics in this, Shakespeare's most profound exploration of England's national and cultural identity

AUTHOR: KATHERINE DUNCAN-JONES

Nicholas Hytner's spectacular period-costume production of Shakespeare's *Henry IV* does not strive too hard for topicality. It is framed, at the opening of *Part One* and the end of *Part Two*, by a spectacle of sidelined, headscarved women wailing as they clutch the dead bodies of fathers, husbands, sons strewn over a stony battlefield. These additions are entirely warranted by the texts. *Part One* opens with the badly "shaken" King resolving on a period of domestic peace before he leads the country to "new broils / To be commenced in

stronds afar remote" – the crusade to Jerusalem that he still dreams of on his deathbed. Likewise, at the end of *Part Two*, the odious Prince John speaks with chilling lightness – "I heard a bird so sing" – of his elder brother's eagerness to take English troops "As far as France". The wailing women remind us once again about the pity of war.

There are a few other "topical" touches. For a matter of seconds, in the closing scene of *Part One*, we see the three defeated rebel leaders dragged onto the stage, bound,

kneeling and wearing pointy black hoods. More trivially, Mistress Quickly's East Cheap Tavern is a fusion of medieval alehouse and modern greasy spoon cafe. This catering anachronism is one of the production's few false notes. Though Falstaff's greed is childishly comic when he scoops leftovers from other people's plates onto his own when he thinks no one is looking, neither the food scraps nor the pottery mugs contribute anything to the larger picture.

Because literal topicality is rarely insisted on, we can enjoy the plays as detailed period pieces which offer contrasts to, as well as analogies with, the way we live now. David Bradley's guilt-ridden King does not in the least remind us of the grinning politicians who recently led us to war. Indeed, he is perhaps more tormented than his lines suggest, showing no trace of the

smooth operator – the bland "king of smiles" – who, as Henry Bolingbroke, forged his way to the crown along "by-paths and indirect crook'd ways". As a result, he seems incapable of recognizing such skills in his eldest son. Their relationship must always appear dysfunctional, but here it seems that the King positively detests him.

Neither Hal's military prowess at the end of *Part One*, nor his patient attempts to spell out his intentions to his dying father at the end of *Part Two*, make a dent in the old man's displaced self-hatred. Even more than usual, this Henry IV seems to be taking part in a different drama from everyone else – a disconnection that is accentuated by Bradley's awkward and mannered verse-speaking.

There are broader and deeper ways in which these Henrys depict an England that we can still recognize.

ABOVE
David Harewood commands the stage as an energetic, charismatic Hotspur

In her delightful anthropological study, *Watching the English: the Hidden Rules of English Behaviour*, Kate Fox chronicles national traits that continue to baffle foreigners, and do not necessarily win us friends.

English habits of superficial politeness can make us seem insincere and lofty, and our deep belief in what Fox nicely labels "the importance of

> *ENGLISH belief in 'the IMPORTANCE of not being earnest' can make us seem INSINCERE and lofty*

KATHERINE DUNCAN-JONES

not being earnest" can be even less appealing. The flippant formulas habitually applied to matters such as death and military conflict – "she's pushing up daisies", "were you in the last show?" – can be read by outsiders who don't "get the tone" as tokens of callousness rather than courage. Appropriately enough at the National Theatre, Hytner's production shows such behaviour patterns to have been fully embedded in the English character during the late Middle Ages, or rather, in the late Elizabethan period. Topical now, these plays were also topical then, with their unsparing presentation of poor rustics being snatched from their villages to be jokily dispatched as "food for powder". Captains would then pocket the dead men's pay, a common malpractice among Elizabeth's troops in Ireland and the Netherlands during the 1590s.

Instead of encouraging the audience to discern some warmth between Hal and Falstaff, Hytner's staging makes it clear from the outset that both men are, like the body doubles of King Henry at the Battle of Shrewsbury, shameless "counterfeits". Matthew Macfadyen is a smooth, rather dislikeable Prince, whose sadistic practical jokes appear recognizably "royal" throughout, and in particular when he humiliates the tapster Francis (Darren Hart), giving him a gratuitous kick in the pants. Though Hal finds Falstaff genuinely funny and wants to emulate his mental and verbal dexterity, it is apparent that he will not mourn for long when he dies. The suggestions of homoeroticism that have lent poignancy to the relationship in other recent productions are avoided. Gambon's habit of rumpling Macfadyen's hair seems no more than faux-fatherly.

The cast is rich in "counterfeits". Only four major characters seem not to be deceivers. Foremost among them is David Harewood's Hotspur, a charismatic warrior whose energy utterly commands the stage while he lives, and who is not easily forgotten. His ability both to gain and to retain the devotion of his much-neglected wife Kate (Naomi Frederick) is for once entirely convincing. It is just a pity that in a text not heavily cut this splendid Hotspur is denied his hasty pre-battle speech to his troops ("O gentlemen, the time of life is short…"). In *Part Two*, Mistress Quickly and Doll Tearsheet (Susan Brown, Eve Myles) evince real warmth in their affection for the dreadful old knight who exploits them.

Their tenderness towards him, earned by nothing beyond the fact that he has been part of their lives for so many years, is affecting. Fourthly, and most surprisingly, Adrian Scarborough's Ned Poins seems blissfully unaware, even in his brief but barbed exchange with Hal about the marital gossip concerning Ned's sister, that he will not ultimately be numbered among the Prince's courtiers.

Harold Bloom once claimed that "Falstaff is a person, while Hal and Hotspur are fictions". Here, on the contrary, Falstaff is the most transparently "false" of all actorly counterfeits. In fact, he embodies that marketing paradox, a genuine fake.

Showing Falstaff as phoney from the outset might appear to risk a diminution of interest, but the effect is the opposite. Michael Gambon's Sir John is fascinating, funny, repulsive and eventually heartbreaking. In *Part One* he carries his big belly lightly as he prances across the vast stage. Some of his speeches are handled lightly, too. Instead of being milked for every second's worth of subversion, in the manner of Orson Welles, the speech on Honour is rattled out extempore, and is all the more persuasive as a result. The Falstaff of the second play is still quick-witted, but health and spirits are failing fast, as Gambon suggests both in face and body. The end is cruel. At the end of *Part Two*, Hal's rejection of his old companion, delivered upstage by a new young King bathed in golden light, seems to induce instant osteoporosis in Falstaff, who bends double like a crushed beetle, mutating before our eyes into one of Larkin's senile Old Fools. That, at least, is not counterfeit. ■

ESSAYS

Kingdom for a knave

Set in a dystopian fascist 1930s London, Richard Loncraine's
adaptation of *Richard III* turns the story of a Machiavellian monarch's
rise and fall into a witty, inventive action-thriller

AUTHOR: PETER HOLLAND

If the producers of *Richard III* had run short of money during filming, they could have tried contacting the tobacco companies. Richard Loncraine's film version comes wreathed in a thick fug of cigar and cigarette smoke. Buckingham (Jim Broadbent) smokes fat cigars, Richard (Ian McKellen) smokes Abdulla cigarettes, which he neatly extracts from his cigarette case and lights one-handed. On the eve of Bosworth, Richard's nervousness and near-mania are sharply defined when he rejects the Stilton and celery and, after pouring a second glass of port, lights one cigarette from the stub of the previous one. Not surprisingly, Catesby, Tyrell and Radcliffe exchange anxious glances.

McKellen's screenplay sets Shakespeare's play in the 1930s, taking its cue from Richard Eyre's production for the National Theatre, which also starred McKellen. Avoiding the cheap paraphernalia of filmic naturalism, the camera is allowed to see the politically incorrect smoking in such quantity, not least because it becomes such an adroit way of indicating character. Authenticity is subordinate to argument. On stage, the action of the play became a history that might

ABOVE
Between Annette
Bening and Maggie
Smith, Robert Downey
Jr is at his preening
best as Rivers, an
American *arriviste*

have happened, an alternative history extrapolating from the perception that the English aristocracy's close potential alignment with fascism could make Richard into an English Hitler. On film, the genre changes. Now, *Richard III* becomes a superb political thriller in an England that is a subtly distorting mirror of reality or a reality adjacent to our own. Loncraine has

eschewed all heritage sites and instead provided an alternative travelogue to a London that is continually displaced. The Bankside power station stands in as a Tower of London far more unnerving than the real one; the government is run from the 1930s architecture of the University of London Senate House; and Edward IV recuperates at Brighton's Royal Pavilion. By avoiding the fake medievalism of conventional representation, Loncraine and McKellen offer a precise cinematic analogy to the Shakespearean history play: a drama that can never offer anything more than a deliberate and self-conscious construction of history, a history that is always aware of the complicities involved in its pretence of being history.

This appears to be the first time that an Anglo-American film version of a Shakespearean history or tragedy has adopted the mode, so overfamiliar in the theatre, of historical transposition. The only parallel I can think of is Christine Ezzard's *As You Like It*, which was set in a modern, depressed Docklands. The disjunction between language and visual style is unremarked and unremarkable.

A dead ringer
for the leader of
the British Union
of Fascists,
Sir Oswald Mosley,
Ian McKellen
steals the show
as Richard III

McKellen has discreetly doctored the text's language, eliminating archaisms in order to prevent a surface obstacle being placed between viewer and film. Shakespeare's Richard's comment to Buckingham, "Cousin, thou wast not wont to be so dull", is, of course, a sharper line than McKellen's version: "Buckingham, you never used to be so dull". But it was the only example that really stopped in my ear. Though, as McKellen states in his introduction to the published screenplay, "*Richard III* is certainly a talkie, in which the words are paramount", he also knows that cinema audiences have a low tolerance of language. If his brilliant stripping of the text retains much of the colloquial in Shakespeare, it has to simplify the opulent rhetoric of the verse to compensate. The characteristic repetitions of the language become singularized, just as characters, too, dovetail and blend into each other; the trio of the Queen's kinsmen, Rivers, Dorset and Gray, distil into one: Robert Downey Jr, superb as Rivers, the 1930s American playboy no longer executed at Pomfret Castle but murdered while in bed with the air-hostess from his transatlantic Pan-Am flight.

Much more significantly, the language is allowed innumerable visual echoes within the action, integrating the film, so that, climactically, Richard screams "A horse, a horse" when his jeep gets stuck in the mud, and we can recall, as a referent for the line, the terrified horses seen moments before, when the military precision turns to chaos as Richard's camp is bombed by Lord Stanley's air force – the significance of Stanley's

RAF uniform throughout the film now finally revealed.

It would be easy to mock the realignments the rehistoricizing creates. But if on stage it would seem excessive to show Lady Anne (Kristin Scott-Thomas) popping pills and, later, shooting up with some tranquillizing drug in the back of a limousine, it is a logical part of film's construction of character in history. Her response to her treatment by Richard is both a detailed and acceptable example of film's psychologizing, and one placed exactly within the context of 1930s behaviour. The substance abuse will metamorphose into the sight of her dead face across which a spider delicately walks, as chilling an effect of cinematic *grand guignol* as anything in Shakespeare's deliberate theatricalizing of Richard's horrors and, in its reminder of Richard as spider, as unequivocal as much in the early verse of Shakespeare's play.

In its blend of stage and screen actors into a coherent cast, *Richard III* is far more successful than Kenneth Branagh's *Henry V* and *Much Ado About Nothing*. Partly, this is because it finds reasons within the conventions of filmic naturalism for its choices, so that Queen Elizabeth (Annette Bening) and Rivers (Downey) are American *arrivistes*, with hints of Mrs Simpson in Bening's excellent performance; their accents are explicable within the film's narrative rather than needing to be ignored like the American presence in Branagh's *Much Ado*. In any case, Bening and Downey are not only comfortable with Shakespeare's language but excited by it, erasing the awful memories of Lawrence Fishburne's *Othello* for Oliver Parker.

But the casting is also successful because the range of styles is a

deliberate reflection of the characters' functions, with Nigel Hawthorne wonderfully wistful as Clarence, first seen as an enthusiastic amateur photographer; Dill Patterson as Ratcliffe, Richard's efficient batman; and Adrian Dunbar as Tyrell, a coalescence of a number of Shakespeare's murderers, a man as ambitiously evil as Richard himself, agreeing to murder the princes as his fingers ponder the choice of chocolates in the Fortnum's selection Richard is holding out to him. The meaningless conjunctions of styles and voices that Branagh has been prepared to accept are here turned into a carefully controlled polyphony.

McKellen has learned from Olivier that Richard's most natural ally is the camera. From the first moment, he looks straight at it, as he announces "And therefore, since I cannot prove a lover, / I am determined to prove a villain"; he cajoles the audience into seeing what he wants to show them. It is a struggle to resist his immense charisma, especially when his nemesis, Richmond, turns out to be such an uneasy cross between a young captain of the school first XV and a man as gung-ho about violence as Richard himself. Loncraine saves his biggest risks for the end, as Richard throws himself off a building just before Richmond can shoot him, and the camera travels down towards a sea of flames – "If not to heaven, then hand in hand to Hell" – all the time staring into Richard's smiling face. As the soundtrack ends the film's sequence of 1930s music with Al Jolson jauntily crooning "I'm sitting on top of the world", Richard's last film predecessor is precisely evoked – Jimmy Cagney screaming "Made it, Ma on top of the world" at the end of *White Heat*. ∎

CRITICAL RESPONSES

Histories

Shakespeare's history plays offer a panoramic survey of a particularly turbulent period of English history, and arguably feature his noblest hero, his most despicable villain and his best-loved comic character

"The great tavern scene [in *Henry IV Part One*] is at once the king-pin of the structure of the play and a parable of Shakespeare's method. In it the main figures … are brought together, reflected, as it were, in the mirror of the imaginations of the Prince and Falstaff…"
JANET SPENS, 1947

"*Henry V* has often been revived (as now) in times of war. Indeed, it was written at such a time, serving to rally national enthusiasm for the hugely expensive and unpopular military expedition to Ireland in the summer of 1599 headed by the Queen's volatile favourite, the Earl of Essex … Major conflicts are often the mothers of cultural innovation. During the First World War, there were at least two productions of the play by all-female casts …"
KATHERINE DUNCAN-JONES, 2003

"A prevailing feature of Shakespeare's earlier work had been the interaction of writers: through co-authorship, borrowing, and conspicuous allusion to their work. The prevailing feature of *Richard II*, however, is the balance of power between men. The distribution of roles here is radically different from *Richard III*. Both are plays about the transfer of the crown, but in the later work it is the interaction of rival claimants that is key. The point is partly to be made through numbers. In *Richard III* the lead speaks 1,116 lines to his challenger's 139; in *Richard II* the King has 749 to Bolingbroke's 399 and York's 280.

Furthermore the characters in *Richard II* are substantial and distinctive, their mode of speech consistent. Crucial moments in the play are driven by conflicting claims for dramatic and personal authority. Patterns of ascent and reversal recur; most graphically they are embodied in the moment at which Bolingbroke and Richard each hold a hand to the crown 'like a deep well / That owes two buckets, filling one another, / The emptier ever dancing in the air, / The other down, unseen and full of water'. This celebrated image of exchange not only escapes rhetorical commonplace, it also encapsulates a dramatic logic that is absent from *Richard II*'s predecessors: the shift in status between members of a group. Along with a remarkable expansion in the diversity of register (from the sonorous grandeur of Carlisle's prophecy to the clipped exactitude of Northumberland's interventions; from the bellicosity of Aumerle to Richard's plaintiveness), this is the innovation of the play as a whole."
BART VAN ES, 2007

"Shakespeare's history plays repeatedly invoke the long shadows cast across the present by legendary figures such as Edward the Black Prince and that 'ever-living man of memory, Henry the Fifth': in the retrospective light of the Shakespeare quatercentenary maybe they have now themselves become that overbearing cultural presence they so memorably dramatize."
EMMA SMITH, 2016

Richard II

R. D. Lancaster

On beds of papers Father snores.
"Death's head," Daughter sneers; cries "God's sake
Kick him." Awake he sighs. She wars
The dark with sword-pointed eyes. "A steak"
He murmurs. "Yes, steak after." She
Nourishes rebellion on
Tasted images, her silk knee
Forced to bow to stage like a don
With Essex to raise up from dead
Documents and paste on the play's
Improbable factions. Her head
Swirls text-full of verse, curls blank maze
Of clues about Tessa and Crow
And Jill and Glossy at the end
Plus the man playing Richard. "Oh
Give Father a poke." She must spend
Five acts between Mother's silent
Distaste for the king's pansiness
And Father's tired non-engagement.
"I know it all" he says. "Words, dress,
Business. I know it off by heart."
Mother: "Does he come on again?
That nasty king?" "The lamb should start
To thaw out soon." "Oh, do explain
What he meant by Antic sits-" "There's
Tessa!" "Heavenly." "You think so?"
"Richard could be worse." "Jill's got shares."
"Actually liking it?" "Oh
Listen to those soldiers. They came
Because it's Shakespeare and they think
The bard's smut." "Chuck 'em- " Trumpets shame
Ice cream. Two generations sink
Under drama. Daughter glares back
At Bolingbroke: admires his rage,
Nose, age, thrust. Father, losing track,
Crumbles dust on his star-crossed stage.

ILLUSTRATION: DARREN SMITH

*A performance of Shakespeare's Richard II,
that story of royal succession and usurpation,
is mirrored (and distorted) in a modern
family drama played out in the stalls.*

Traged

ies

ESSAYS

Man or monster

The late tragedy *Coriolanus* has polarized critical opinion since its inception, the all-too-human frailties of its eponymous hero drawing praise and dismissal in equal measure, as shown in this classic assessment from 1922

AUTHOR: JOHN MIDDLETON MURRY

The general opinion of criticism is curiously reluctant to crystallize about *Coriolanus*. Is it because *Coriolanus* is perhaps the most neglected of Shakespeare's greater plays? Or is the play neglected because of the indecision it provokes? The divergence of opinion about it is extraordinary. Mr Lytton Strachey, for instance, has lately declared that "rhetoric, enormously magnificent and extraordinarily elaborate is the beginning and the middle and the end of *Coriolanus*. The hero is not a human being at all". Mr Bernard Shaw, on the other hand, puts Coriolanus with Faulconbridge in *King John* as "admirable descriptions of instinctive temperaments", and says, with intelligible paradox, that "the play of *Coriolanus* is the greatest of Shakespeare's comedies". It has been also lately maintained that *Coriolanus* is Shakespeare's most perfect work of art.

Divergence of this kind does not in the least resemble the recent controversy as to whether *Hamlet* is an aesthetic success or an aesthetic failure. All the world, and not least those particular disputants, is agreed that *Hamlet* is a mighty work; its precise degree of perfection alone is in debate; its greatness is admitted. Quite otherwise with *Coriolanus*. Nobody seems quite certain if it is a great play or not, and it is so seldom performed that there is no consensus of popular opinion as to its dramatic merits. The reason why it is so seldom performed is that the theme is unsympathetic to the ordinary man, who cannot accept as a tragic hero one whose ungovernable pride forces him to become a renegade. It is to this instinctive sentiment that Mr Shaw gives paradoxical expression when he says that *Coriolanus* is the greatest of Shakespeare's comedies. Coriolanus is human enough, but he is so human that we are angry with him for not behaving more sensibly; we do not feel that his conduct is inevitable, like Othello's; we prefer to say that

it is natural. By one burst of temper he exiles himself from Rome, by a second he kills himself. Nothing is changed in him – as he was at the beginning of the play so he is at the end. Whereas the tragic hero deserves to die, Coriolanus does not. A hero of great Shakespearean tragedy deserves to die because we cannot conceive him continuing to live. But the death of Coriolanus is a shock to us; we are not surprised that Shakespeare scamped it and, by making Aufidius repent it on the instant, turned it into an accident. To put the matter irreverently, Coriolanus is a big schoolboy; Molière might have disposed of him better than Shakespeare.

Still, not even Molière could have made him live as Shakespeare has. To say, as Mr Strachey says, that he is not a human being at all, is indeed remarkable. He is, of course, a being of a quite different kind from the heroes of the great tragedies; but he is more of the human being than they. Compared with Antony, it is true, he is almost thin-blooded; but who is not thin and unsubstantial compared to that king of men? In his own play and his own setting Coriolanus is absolutely convincing. He is not so complete a man as Antony; he inhabits a sphere of more primitive development, but within that sphere he is fixed as solid as a rock. Coriolanus is Shakespeare's Homeric hero; and it is largely because of the competences with which he is presented that this tragic end becomes perfunctory. That such a man should meet with a violent end is too natural to be inevitable; his death is a physical rather than a spiritual consummation. To give it a spiritual significance Shakespeare needed to employ another Iago, to arrange the toils into which the instinctive man must fall. But there was no Iago in the story. It is true he might have made Aufidius into one. At the beginning, indeed, he seems to have intended to. Aufidius's speech at the end of the first act –

> Mine emulation
> Hath not that honour in't it had: for where
> I thought to crush him in an equal force.
> True sword to sword. I'll potch at him some
> way,
> Or wrath or craft may get him

puts an Iago before us; but Shakespeare

Coriolanus is HUMAN enough ... so human that we are ANGRY with HIM for not behaving more sensibly

JOHN MIDDLETON MURRY

could not hold him to his task. Aufidius, too, at the critical moment becomes the instinctive Homeric hero.

Aufidius is the weak point of the play. Dramatically, his function is to play in the second part of the drama the role held by Sicinius and Brutus, the Tribunes, in the first, but to play it with more steadiness of hatred even than they, because Aufidius has to compass Coriolanus's death, while the Tribunes need only his exile. But whereas the Tribunes play their part to the life, and we know and follow and comprehend their every move in entangling Coriolanus in his own weakness, Aufidius is as impulsive as Coriolanus himself, and as evidently incapable of plotting as he. Instead of being plainer to us than Sicinius and Brutus, he becomes ten times as shadowy.

But Coriolanus is magnificent, and insofar as he is the play the play is magnificent also. He is Plato's man of impulse to the life. When his wounds are mentioned we see the schoolboy blush, with more of vanity than true modesty in it, come to his face. He cannot remember the name of the man of Corioli for whose freedom he begs. "Marcius, his name?" asks Lartius.

> By Jupiter, forgot!
> I am weary; yea, my memory is tired.
> Have we no wine here?

Was the physical man ever more swiftly presented? Coriolanus knows nothing of himself. His consciousness, his memory, his purpose – these are all in the keeping of his mother, Volumnia, or Menenius. His mind is sharp and his eye clear only on the battlefield. When he turns away from it, he is bewildered and lost in a strange country. He cannot notice

BELOW
Ralph Fiennes in the lead role of the 2011 film adaptation of *Coriolanus,* his directorial debut

things or people; he barely recognizes his wife whom he loves. The idea that he should behave in the city with the same circumspection with which he orders a battle or takes in a town is quite incomprehensible to him; when his mother suggests it, he cannot understand. It is Volumnia, not he, who has the Consulship in mind when he returns victorious; for plans beyond the battlefield his mind is an abeyance. He does what he is told, like a reluctant child; and, after the fatal outburst of his anger, he is hopeless and pathetic; he feels his mother has deserted him.

> I muse my mother
> Does not approve me further, who was wont
> To call them swollen vassals.

And he returns, after much persuasion, to make amends like a child, repeating the key word of his conduct in case he should forget it. "The word is mildly." Past and future have no existence for him. He remembers only what he feels, the burning glow of an insult that has not been revenged; and not till he sees his mother and his wife before him has he an inkling that he is committing an act of shame that is threatening his own city, Rome, with fire and sword. Till that moment Rome is no more than the cause of his insult. At the last, with one of those amazing strokes of whose sheer simplicity lesser writers are ever afraid, Shakespeare makes him turn on Aufidius.

> *Auf.* Name not the God, thou boy of tears!
> *Cor.* Ha!
> *Auf.* No more.
> *Cor.* Measureless liar, thou hast made my heart
> Too great for what contains it. Boy! O slave!
> Pardon me, lords, 'tis the first time that ever
> I was forced to scold.

The first time! It is hopeless. Coriolanus is lost in time. Shakespeare's Coriolanus sees neither before nor after. He is ignorant of his own nature as a savage. How should the man who cried: "'Tis the first time that I was ever forced to scold" know the hidden workings of his own heart? His purposes loom on him only when they are being accomplished. And surely Shakespeare has taken care that we shall understand him, without our being compelled to invent processes of mind for him; surely, the vital words are the last which Coriolanus speaks to his mother, wife and friends when he leaves the gates of Rome.

While I remain above the ground you shall
Hear from me still, and never of me aught
But what is like me formerly.

Is not that tragic irony of the highest kind? The monstrous thing that Coriolanus is to do is "like him formerly". He who knows nothing of himself may mean it as Menenius understood it, "That's worthily"; but we, who have watched his blind, angry blundering bring to naught the deliberate purposes his friends have for a moment fixed upon him, know that the former self, like which he will remain, is a thing of impulse only, of pride and anger and resentment and courage. The Tribunes provoked him and he tried to kill them; Rome has provoked him and he tried to kill it. We know; he does not; and he is far more surprised than we are to find himself entering Antium. His brief soliloquy – his only one in the play – gives us the exact measure and quality of his surprise. "O world, thy slippery turns!" It seems to him odd and strange that he should be seeking out Aufidius.

So, fellest foes
Whose passions and whose plots have broke
their sleep
To take the one the other, by some chance,
Some trick not worth an egg, shall grow dear
friends
And interjoin their issues.

The incredible change in his actions is to him just the result of "some trick not worth an egg". He cannot understand it; he can see no more of himself than his actions; and when, confronted with Aufidius, he finds that his actions need some explanation, he instinctively reshapes the immediate past to his purpose. The friends who have tried to protect him and to prevent his suicide, who have offered to share his exile, suddenly become "the dastard nobles / Who have all forsook me". True, that is in Plutarch. But what Shakespeare has done is what Plutarch could never do – to put before us the living man whose thought and words were ever the servants of his impulses alone.

Coriolanus is the drama, and since he is perfectly presented, the drama is all but perfect. But the weakness of Aufidius remains, and we cannot help speculating how Shakespeare came to fumble with him. Perhaps we may suggest the cause. In Plutarch's story, Aufidius appears on the scene only after Coriolanus has been exiled. We imagine that when Shakespeare first read through the story in Thomas North's translation and shaped it as a drama in his mind, he had a clear conception of the part Aufidius was to play as the man of hate and conspiracy. When he came to write the play, with his eyes fixed even more closely upon North's book than they had been during the writing of *Antony and Cleopatra* a year before, he followed his own

conception of Aufidius during the first act. There was nothing in North to change it; Aufidius simply did not appear. But when he reached Coriolanus's exile, and Aufidius made his entry into North, he found a different Aufidius from the one he had conceived. Instead of a man poisoned by jealousy, he found a chivalrous enemy, "a man of great minde". Plutarch's Aufidius is said, indeed, to hate Coriolanus; but it is the hate of one enemy for another; and there is something sportsmanlike, schoolboyish even, in their rivalry: "Many times in battels where they met, they were ever at the encounter one against another, like lusty courageous youths, striving in all emulation of honour." To this suggestion Shakespeare unconsciously succumbed, at a moment when he was following North's language more closely than ever. He forgot the Aufidius he had presented two long acts ago, the Aufidius who had declared his nature thus:

My valour's poison'd
With only suffering stain by him …
Where I find him, were it
At home upon my brother's guard, even there
Against the hospitable canon, would I
Wash my fierce hand in's heart …

Instead of this, Aufidius now becomes Coriolanus's impulsive counterpart. Shakespeare gives him a magnificent speech:

Know thou first
I loved the maid I married; never man
Sigh'd truer breath; but that I see thee here
Thou noble thing! more dances my rapt heart
Than when I first my wedded mistress saw
Bestride my threshhold.

There is no hint of Aufidius's wonderful words in North. But Shakespeare could not resist North's suggestion of "the emulation of honour". The noble rivalry still exists. And yet, when he first presented Aufidius he had used that very phrase to show that Aufidius's nobility was a thing of the past. "Mine emulation / Hath not that honour in't it had." But the temptation was too great. Back comes all the honour to Aufidius's emulation. We are given a moving and magnificent scene. But the two Aufidiuses can never now be reconciled. The poisoned plotter has to carry on the action of the play to its tragic end; but it is the generous opponent who lives in our minds, the man who could no more have suborned assassins to murder Coriolanus than he could have resisted Coriolanus's swift appeal: "Pray you, / Stand to me in this cause." All through the fifth act we feel that Shakespeare does not know what to do with Aufidius and in the final scene the conflict of the two characters who bear one name is manifest and unresolved. Aufidius has deliberately plotted Coriolanus's murder, and played even more cold-bloodedly than the Tribunes upon his temper to sting him to an outburst. Suddenly, he changes parts again. He becomes the chivalrous enemy.

> My rage is gone,
> And I am struck with sorrow.

CORIOLANUS is the drama, and since he is perfectly presented, the DRAMA is all but PERFECT

JOHN MIDDLETON MURRY

To some, perhaps, this attempted analysis of the actual working of Shakespeare's mind in the construction of *Coriolanus* on the basis of North's story may appear fanciful; but we believe it gives a coherent psychological explanation of that radical duality in the conception of Aufidius which has been noticed by many critics before.

But it is impossible to leave it at that. At one moment, at least, Shakespeare spent all the force of his poetic genius on putting an heroic Aufidius before us, in his speech of welcome to Coriolanus; and Shakespeare was not in the habit of shrinking from "unpleasant tasks": he did not flinch from Iago. When we remember that two acts and a half intervene between the first presentation of Aufidius's character and his reappearance; that at the time of his reappearance Shakespeare was working with an eye glued to the book; and that the phrase "emulation of honour" had been as it were a keyword that stuck in his brain from his first reading of North – then, we believe, it becomes clear that under the immediate influence of North, Shakespeare reverted to a conception of Aufidius which had been dismissed to the past by Aufidius's speech in Act 1, scene 10, and which was inconsistent with his original idea of the dramatic action of the play. Then, perhaps, we may value Aufidius's speech in Act 4, scene 5, as something more than the most splendid piece of poetry in a play full of splendid poetry as a precise indication of when and how and for what cause Shakespeare's human instincts triumphed over his deliberate artistic purposes.

Of the other characters there is little that is new to be said. But there is a correspondence in the play which seems to have escaped attention though it reveals the subtlety of Shakespeare's characterization. At the very beginning of the first scene he suggests the strange relation between Coriolanus and his mother. "Though soft-conscienced men," says the First Citizen, "can be content to say it was for his country, he did it to please his mother and to be partly proud." We call this nowadays the Oedipus complex. But what is amazing is the way Shakespeare conveys that Coriolanus and Volumnia together are one being – Volumnia the mind and purpose, Coriolanus the body and strength. Hence the peculiar subtlety of his creation of Virgilia. There is really no place for her; if she is to be given at all, she must be given in a hundred words. Shakespeare does it with an instinctive gesture. But Virgilia is a being apart. The real and binding unity is between mother and son. And at the same moment Shakespeare makes them use the same phrase. When Coriolanus has been banished, Volumnia in a frenzy of rage waylays the Tribunes, and cries:

> I would my son
> Were in Arabia and thy tribe before him,
> His good sword in his hand.

When Coriolanus is at bay in Antium in the final scene, he also cries:

> O that I had him
> With six Aufidiuses, or more, his tribe,
> To use my lawful sword.

Whether the repetition was deliberate, calculated art, who can tell? It does not matter, for if it was not calculated, it is only one more proof of Shakespeare's astonishing instinctive realization of a blood-bond of temper. ∎

When Julius Caesar is murdered at the Capitol in Rome, on the Ides of March, his assassins leave the loyal Mark Antony to lament alone over his corpse – and to prophesy the chaos to come. "Ate" here refers ominously to the Greek goddess of recklessness and ruin.

"Thou art ruins noblest ever live tide of

the
of the
man That
d in the
times "

Julius Caesar, act 3, scene 1

ANTONY O, pardon me, thou bleeding piece of earth,
That I am meek and gentle with these butchers!
Thou art the ruins of the noblest man
That ever lived in the tide of times.
Woe to the hand that shed this costly blood!
Over thy wounds now do I prophesy,
Which, like dumb mouths, do ope their ruby lips,
To beg the voice and utterance of my tongue
A curse shall light upon the limbs of men;
Domestic fury and fierce civil strife
Shall cumber all the parts of Italy;
Blood and destruction shall be so in use
And dreadful objects so familiar
That mothers shall but smile when they behold
Their infants quarter'd with the hands of war;
All pity choked with custom of fell deeds:
And Caesar's spirit, ranging for revenge,
With Ate by his side come hot from hell,
Shall in these confines with a monarch's voice
Cry 'Havoc,' and let slip the dogs of war;
That this foul deed shall smell above the earth
With carrion men, groaning for burial.

Doctor in the house Hamlet

Courtyard Theatre, Stratford-upon-Avon, 2008

Sci-fi TV series luminaries David Tennant and Patrick Stewart headed a suitably stellar cast in Gregory Doran's modern-dress staging of the ultimate revenge tragedy

AUTHOR: EMMA SMITH

The most arresting moment in Gregory Doran's RSC *Hamlet*? Not a soliloquy, although David Tennant makes a remarkable job of his first one, foetal in private agony. Not the ghost, who, despite an edgy opening scene with powerful searchlights probing the darkened audience and stage, fails to convince. Not Hamlet's death in the arms of a Horatio whose lines, like those of Fortinbras, are cut to focus on the tragic spectacle. Perhaps surprisingly, the moment when the production seems most confident and inventive is the dumbshow before "The Mousetrap". The Player King and Queen are a grotesque pair, he dwarfish with monkey ears, shuffling on boots attached to his knees, she fleshily transvestite with bare breasts and whitened face. The villainous Lucianus snakes down from the flies, muscular and bare-torsoed, sporting a heart-shaped spangled codpiece he later unzips to reveal a flopping spring. The murdered King is covered with a white sheet and

ABOVE
Hamlet and Ophelia
(Mariah Gale) watch
the play within a play

winched into the air, hovering like a cartoon ghost.

This play brought by the travelling troupe to Elsinore is designedly retro, with haughty rhymed verse preceded by a dumbshow in the style of Norton and Sackville's *Gorboduc*, already two generations old by the time of *Hamlet*'s first performances. As such, it is key to the play's sustained nostalgia – familial, political, religious and theatrical. Rather than being purely instrumental, here it offers a real insight into why Hamlet is so preoccupied by theatre and by acting. In a beautifully executed vignette, Tennant, atop a wicker costume hamper, falteringly recalls the speech on "rugged Pyrrhus", prompted by the players. The words return haltingly from his memory: "coagulate gore" is an old favourite. This Hamlet, who

seems, as we do, quickly to lose sight of his father's commands to "remember" and "revenge", instead unpacks his mind of much-loved theatrical speeches, in an affection for theatre both sincere and without condescension.

What is so compelling about the dumbshow's freakish depiction is the ways in which only its plot – not its characters – mimics what the Ghost has told us. This production has no truck with the oversexed Gertrude of Hamlet's fevered imagination – no "reechy kisses" pass between her and Claudius, although numerous well-observed details suggest that theirs is a mutual and loving relationship. Penny Downie's Gertrude steps in to supply "Wittenberg" to prompt the new stepfather addressing the student prince in Act 1, scene 2, and she

greets the news that Fortinbras has been brought to diplomatic terms with real relief and pride in her husband's political abilities. Her counterpart in "Gonzago" is her pantomimic obverse, just as the Player King confounds the noble opinion in which old Hamlet is held, and Claudius's exit is less guilt-stricken than calmly

> ❝
> *Tennant's HAMLET is rather like his Doctor – sardonic, clever, verbally facile, isolated – but less mordantly intellectual*
>
> EMMA SMITH

disappointed in the flippant prince. The idea, however, that the players' welcome intervention in the Danish court has been irreversibly catalytic is firmly established. After the rout of the performance, Hamlet lolls on the throne wearing the abandoned play-crown at a rakish angle, before heading to his mother's closet and to the murder of Polonius. Everything has changed.

That an old play might be electrified in a new context is, of course, an appropriate conceit for this much-hyped production of *Hamlet*. Tennant's television role as the Time Lord Doctor Who and as Hamlet has dominated media coverage – and ticket sales – as an irresistibly unlikely coupling of high and low culture. In fact Tennant's Hamlet is rather like his Doctor – sardonic, clever, verbally facile, isolated – but less mordantly intellectual and more febrile. Doctor Who's superciliousness as he bests circumstances and challengers in episode after episode here gives way to a radical susceptibility. Hamlet's loneliness is not that of superior understanding but of submission to events. His belated realization that "the readiness is all" seems here less an intellectually achieved stoicism, more a visceral understanding that he is the object rather than agent of events. Skinny and exophthalmic, he evinces an inner torture which we observe rather than fully understand: as the production matures, it will be more possible to judge whether this opacity is its weakness or its signal insight. Barefoot, in red T-shirt and Levis much of the time, his youth is always prominent. He is largely likeable – flusteredly unable to respond to Ophelia, rather than violent,

a teenage puritan rather than a would-be Nero in his mother's closet. The Ghost's presence in this scene draws out a poignant family portrait: parents sit on the bed, with husband tenderly touching wife's hair, and the child kneeling at their feet in an idealized lost innocence strikingly devoid of that psychosexual knowingness with which the scene seems often to be freighted.

This Hamlet can be funny, too: whistling with concentrated sobriety an off-key "Three Blind Mice" as a national anthem plays at court; guying Osric or Polonius (Oliver Ford Davies) with nervy, restless verbal facility; upstaging the King with a "wheeeeee" as he scoots away, after his arrest for Polonius's

murder, strapped with duct tape into an office chair. This makes for a more extended comic strain in the play, into which Polonius's laboured rhetoric falls happily, as does the northern Gravedigger (Mark Hadfield), wheezing with mordant mirth as he shovels skulls from beneath the stage.

Robert Jones's design has a reflective floor and backdrop, emphasizing the play's theme of surveillance, although only the splintered spider's web in this modern arras, dominating the second half as a marker of Polonius's murder, makes visual capital from its setting.

Neither Laertes's transformation from callow student to hard man with leather jacket and pistol, nor Ophelia's maniacal dancing dispensing misidentified foliage is truly convincing, despite the production's particular sympathy for their father.

All eyes in this production are on Tennant – and his energetic and fresh performance deserves the attention. But there is also a quiet, controlled counter to his narrative of filial and regal dispossession: Claudius. In Patrick Stewart's stilly, bespectacled King, we get not the silkily smiling villain but something infinitely more troubling: an essentially decent man, whose offence is like bile in his throat. He accepts the poisoned cup from Hamlet with equable grace, knowing his time is up, and his final movements as he lies dying on the floor are to reach out to his queen. In its thoughtful depiction of Claudius, Doran's production actually gestures towards that play in which the son of the murdered king is marginalized and the murderer himself takes centre stage: *Macbeth*. ∎

DIALOGUES

En garde!

Six Shakespeare devotees put on their bookies' hats to discuss the fencing duel between Hamlet and Laertes. In what form were the combatants, and were the odds against the Prince of Denmark winning fair?

AUTHORS: FRANK KERMODE, ANTHONY HOLDEN, ROBIN MARRIS, KEN FOLLETT, LINDEN STAFFORD AND DANIEL MARCIANO

A sporting correspondence between Frank Kermode (literary critic), Anthony Holden (Shakespeare biographer, poker-player and rapporteur), Robin Marris (economist), Ken Follett (novelist), Linden Stafford (Arden editor) and Daniel Marciano (fencing instructor).

FRANK KERMODE Looking for problems to talk about in a lecture, I lit upon the duel at the end of Hamlet. Relaying Claudius's challenge to Hamlet, Osric tells him that the King has "laid on twelve for nine" (in terms of "hits") in favour of Laertes. But nobody (including Arden editor Harold Jenkins, in an extremely long note) seems to have figured out the odds. You, Tony, may be able to do so, after all those sweaty nights playing poker in Las Vegas. Quite a problem, I warn you. But you will handle it.

ANTHONY HOLDEN You're right. This is complex, not least because the text is ambiguous. But here goes: by my reckoning, the odds on Laertes beating Hamlet are lousy for the punter: to wit, 1:4 (or 4 to 1 on in bookie-speak). Not much of a bet, even if Laertes is as good as reported,

ABOVE
Kenneth Branagh takes up arms in his 1996 adaptation of *Hamlet*

and Hamlet has, as he says, been forgoing all custom of exercise. But I think that's our boy playing football coach-style "mind games". For the form guide also tells us he's been "in constant practice" since Laertes went into France (ie, at the start of the play, ie, while he himself has recently been at Elsinore). That may just be Shakespeare nodding. If Hamlet wins

against the odds, we may need a Stewards' Enquiry…

How do I work that out? Osric says that the King hath laid that in a dozen passes Hamlet shall not exceed three hits: "He hath laid on twelve for nine." (Note the Bard's brilliant use of that technical word "on".) Twelve for nine equals four for three, would appear to mean 4:3. But the King seems to be cheating already.

"Exceeding" three hits surely means making four out of a possible twelve. Four hits in twelve equals at least one in three, or one in four in betting terms, ergo the odds are 1/4 – four to one – on Laertes, or 4:1 against Hamlet.

Is Osric, however, not really a betting man? Has he misunderstood his instructions, ie, the King's wager? If we make an enticing textual amendment (in this prose passage, which doesn't have to scan), "the King hath laid that in a dozen passes Hamlet shall not exceed BY three hits", it changes everything, and the odds improve (from Claudius's point of view) to 4:3. Still a bad bet, however, so he might need to fix the rapiers.

If not Osric's error, then the typesetter's? I am using the Las Vegas edition, of course, whereas

Facing front, Laurence Olivier starred in and directed this film version in 1948

Arden omits the word wager at 205, ie, Horatio says merely "You will lose, my lord". Hamlet, as we know, replies, "I shall win at the odds". So even Wittenberg University's Horatio (if not our hero) has got as muddled as Osric by all this; it is, of course, the King who will lose the wager, not Hamlet, if Hamlet wins the duel.

So maybe Arden's Jenkins, who made the logical deletion of wager, knew whereof he spake, ie, fancied a bit of a flutter?

FK But what about the six Barbary horses and the six swords? And the king's "I do not fear it, I have seen you both"? Moreover, the great Evert Sprinchorn, so rudely dismissed by Jenkins, shows by means of binomial coefficients (which I confess I do not understand) that the answer to the question "Given a bout between equally able players, A and B, that is to continue until either A has won eight games or B has won five, what are the odds against A?" (ie, the odds against A represent the odds Laertes is accepting in the unequal match in which he is considered Hamlet's superior) is that the probability of A's winning turns out to be 794/4096. Expressed as odds, this is approximately 4:1 against Laertes. This is the answer that would have satisfied Fermat and Pascal, who first began to consider probabilities. So?

AH These conclusions seem to be about Laertes winning despite the handicap imposed by Claudius – ie, I suspect (though I understand Sprinchorn no better than you) that we are into the realms of probability rather than mere odds.

Otherwise, it is deeply gratifying that, by such erudite means, you

have reached the same conclusion I ground out in the first place. That said, I think I'd better run this by an economist I know...

ROBIN MORRIS The King says that Hamlet's maximum scoring rate is one in four (three in twelve). But he could do worse. Therefore Hamlet is, say, 5:1 against. The other chap is 1:5 on.

AH Thank you. Very helpful. Time to bring in the novelist Ken Follett, who (like me) will go pretty much anywhere, anytime to see any production of *Hamlet*.

KEN FOLLETT This isn't a money bet. Claudius has staked six Barbary horses, and Laertes has staked six French rapiers and poniards, with their assigns, and so on. There are no odds in the bookmaking sense. The numbers refer to something else.

Everyone assumes Hamlet is the inferior swordsman. Therefore Laertes must be given a handicap. The size of the handicap is what is under discussion.

When Horatio says "You will lose this wager", Hamlet replies, "I shall win at the odds". Hamlet has not placed a bet, of course. He expects to win the contest, given the handicap. The agreed handicap is three hits. If Laertes scores a minimum of three hits more than Hamlet, Laertes wins the match. If he does better than Hamlet by a smaller margin, he nevertheless loses the match.

After that, it gets muddled. Claudius has laid that, in a dozen passes, Laertes shall not exceed Hamlet three hits. But what is a pass? Logically, a pass would end with a hit. In a dozen passes, there would be a total of twelve hits. But in that case it would be impossible to win

ABOVE
Maxine Peake at the Royal Exchange Theatre in 2014

by three. The only possible scores are: 12-0 (Laertes wins by twelve points), 11-1 (Laertes wins by ten points), 10-2 (eight), 9-3 (six), 8-4 (four), 7-5, (two) 6-6 (a draw). The arithmetic is no different if each pass consists of two hits, giving a maximum of twenty-four. You still can't win by an odd number.

However, in the fight itself, in what seems to be the third pass, each wounds the other; so it must be possible to have more than one hit per pass. On reflection, that might have been common, as the two combatants might frequently touch one another more or less simultaneously. On the other hand, more than two hits per pass is unlikely. So perhaps each pass includes either one or two hits, and Claudius figures the maximum number of hits is twenty-four, and the minimum twelve. In that case there are six possible ways to win by three hits: 13-10 (anything higher gives a total of more than twenty-four hits), 12-9, 11-8, 10-7, 9-6, 8 5 (anything lower gives a total of fewer than twelve hits). Laertes also wins, by four points or more, if he scores more than thirteen, and if Hamlet scores four or fewer. Hamlet wins if the score is 13-11, 12-10, and so on down to 7-5. But Osric ignores these possibilities, focusing on the narrowest allowable victory, for clarity.

But why does Osric say that Claudius has laid on twelve for nine, when this score is only one of six ways to win by three points? Was it just an illustration?

PS: Is it possible that a bout could end in a no-score draw (hence Osric's line at 305, "Nothing neither way")? In this reading it is the fourth bout that sees the guys wounding each other. Is it possible that Claudius is betting that at no point in the bouts will Laertes exceed Hamlet's score by three hits, at 4-1, for example, or 6-3. "He hath laid on twelve for nine" – but Claudius is betting against Laertes and on Hamlet so is the King running a book on the side? Or did Shakespeare screw up?

PPS: Claudius does have a side bet of sorts, staking "an union" that Hamlet will win if he should give the first or second hit, or if he should "quit in answer of the third exchange". What could this mean?

Of course, there was never any real WAGER, since the object of the DUEL was to kill HAMLET

LINDEN STAFFORD

FK: Union can mean a pearl. But he means to dissolve it in the wine to poison Hamlet. Shakespeare simply put in as many betting deals as he could think of.

Follett, for all his industry, must surely be wrong about simultaneous hits. And in any case the two-hit exchange manifestly couldn't be considered part of a formal duel.

AH Quite, but Follett's ingenuity also suggests that we must find out what is meant by a "pass". I'm asking Richard Cohen, Olympic fencer and author of *By the Sword*, to consult a fencing-master…

DANIEL MARCIANO A pass seems to be what the French call *une phrase d'armes*, in as much as fencing is a conversation. For instance, an attack followed by a parry and reply and possibly a counter-reply until the fencers are again out of reach. A *phrase d'armes* in a modern fencing bout may end up with neither of the two fencers being hit or a hit. Let's not talk about a double hit as though it were a modern bout; in the old times it was pleasantly called "le coup des deux veuves". "Une veuve" is a widow. In Shakespeare's language, a pass should come to an end when one of the fencers is hit.

AH Cohen and Marciano have passed on the entire correspondence to Linden Stafford, currently working on the new Arden edition of *Hamlet*.

LINDEN STAFFORD I can't speak for the *Hamlet* editors, Ann Thompson and Neil Taylor, who have yet to hand me their commentary on the duel. Harold Jenkins's very long note, while accepting that the text is flawed and internally contradictory, suggests a

"divided intent" on Shakespeare's part between the number of passes and the method of scoring. Of course, there was never any real wager, since the object of the duel was to kill Hamlet, and, failing a hit with the envenomed tip, the poisoned chalice was to have settled the final score. The business of the Barbary horses and French rapiers is merely window-dressing to persuade Hamlet that Claudius has set up a genuine friendly match.

As WS was obviously busy plotting the duel scene, and how the King would entrap Hamlet, it's most likely that he threw together a few terms such as "pass", "bout" and "hit", and sexed up the entirely bogus "wager" with Osric's blether of "six Barbary horses, against the which he has impawned, as I take it, six French rapiers and poniards, with their assigns" to distract Hamlet from discovering his impending death. After Osric's first announcement, "My lord, his majesty bade me signify to you that 'a has laid a great wager on your head", there are not only many lines but also many golden words spent by Osric before he gets to the big question, "He hath laid on twelve for nine, and it would come to immediate trial if your lordship would vouchsafe the answer". It hardly matters what the courtly messenger actually says, as long as it sounds elaborate enough to stop Hamlet from guessing that there is no wager. I've always thought he seems to fall for it too easily, apart from feeling ill around his heart with a kind of gain-giving as would perhaps trouble a woman. But that's Hamlet for you.

AH Quite. Thanks to all. File now closed. After Frank Kermode has given his lecture, I will offer the problem to readers of the *TLS*. ∎

CRITICAL RESPONSES

Tragedies

Drawing heavily on classical myth and legend, Shakespeare's
tragedies boast protagonists who are essentially
good but whose weaknesses prove to be their downfall

"Like its main character, *King Lear* is absolute and imperious; its readers submit like subjects. Keats's plain infinitive in the title of his poem 'On Sitting Down To Read *King Lear* Once Again' becomes, as he reads, a two-fold transfiguration. He is compelled to 'burn through' the play, and both reader and text are 'consumed in the fire'. Down the centuries, the greatest of critics have had to bend the knee, often describing the play's conquest of the intellect in terms of physical submission. (Dr Johnson: 'So powerful is the current of the poet's imagination that the mind which once ventured within it is hurried irresistibly along'; Schlegel: 'But who could possibly enumerate all the different combinations and situations by which our minds are here as it were stormed by the poet?') The play's hold over the intellect is accepted: its demand on the heart – on what might be called our moral vanity – is often rejected. Poor Tom's physical nakedness is matched by the moral nakedness of many of the characters. Reduced to appetite, the human being is a fleshy automaton jerked by the need to copulate or kill. Lear's question about Poor Tom sums up the play's philosophical basis as a threat: 'Is man no more than this?'"
OLIVER REYNOLDS, 1995

"*Othello* is almost a copybook demonstration of what happens when trust and suspicion come into contact. Othello, like David in the Hebrew Bible, is a foreigner to introspection; he is what he does and what he can relate. His way of speaking is not to argue but to tell a story – to the senators of Venice as much as to his future wife… Othello, like the oral storyteller he is, tells a tale; Iago, like a novelist, sums up a character in two words, 'erring barbarian', 'supersubtle Venetian'. The play charts the way in which Iago's language gradually infects that of Othello and how, when that happens, Othello is doomed. That is true; but it also charts the way in which the language of a culture of suspicion infects the language of a culture of trust. Iago sows the seeds of suspicion in Othello's mind by asking him to *interpret*, to get to the bottom of things. The ancient tragedian and the oral storyteller answer the question: what happened? The novelist and the modern playwright answer the question: what *really* happened? A small difference, it might be thought, but, in effect, a monumental one."
GABRIEL JOSIPOVICI, 1997

"It is hard to think of a moment in a Shakespeare play when justice is done. In *Titus Andronicus*, Titus complains that Astraea, the goddess of justice, has abandoned the Earth. He has good reason to complain: his daughter has been raped, and her hands cut off and tongue cut out to prevent her from identifying her assailants. In *King Lear*, Gloucester complains, 'As flies to wanton boys are we to th' gods. / They kill us for their sport'. Friar Lawrence in *Romeo and Juliet* is cleared of murdering the lovers, but the Montagus and Capulets are surely responsible for their deaths, and they will go unpunished. What we mainly find in Shakespeare are stories of injustice."
DAVID WOOTTON, 2014

Macbeth
Roy Fuller

"Fillet of a fenny snake,
In the cauldron boil and bake."
Did the witch intend to say
Boil the liquid quite away,
Then go on applying heat
Till the thing is fit to eat?
Why then not put in that skillet
All the snake not just the fillet?
Which is worse, the poetry
Or the careless recipe?

Who would imagine making salad were
At all to do with poetry and death?
And yet what peeled and cut the beetroot are
The guilty frightening fingers of Macbeth.

"Light thickens; and the crow
Makes wings to th' rooky wood."
Nobody seems to know
If the lines are bad or good.
Some think in those few words
Are too many darkling birds.
But it might have marred the book
Had Shakespeare said "the rook
Makes wings to th' crowy wood."

ILLUSTRATION: DARREN SMITH

---

*Shakespeare's language in Macbeth,
starting with the witches' incantations, can
be both striking and somewhat bizarre –
as this poem irreverently suggests*

Contro

versies

Shall I compare thee?

Portraits of Shakespeare have long been a source of controversy. A *TLS* review of the National Portrait Gallery's exhibition 'Searching for Shakespeare' set off a chain of responses from Shakespeare scholars

ILLUSTRATION: NOMA BAR

MARCH 31, 2006

The review by Katherine Duncan-Jones of the Searching for Shakespeare exhibition catalogue (March 17) was wrong to suggest that the Chandos portrait is not of the period because it is painted on canvas. The 1590s and 1600s were a turning point for British artists in the use of paint surfaces, and canvas became increasingly popular for artists at this date as a far more practical alternative to wooden panels, which needed to be joined together. A short visit to the Tudor and Jacobean galleries at the National Portrait Gallery will make this point: ten portraits from the period are on canvas (as are others in the exhibition, including the probable portrait of Richard Burbage).

Duncan-Jones describes the feigned oval as an "unlikely feature" of the date 1600, despite the fact that several other feigned ovals of around this date are illustrated in the catalogue, including the John Donne portrait of c1595.

Tarnya Cooper

APRIL 7, 2006

Tarnya Cooper says that I am "wrong" to question the 1600-1610 date attached to the Chandos portrait. But all the portraits discussed in Dr Cooper's essay on "Portrait Painting in England around 1600" are on wood panel, while "Chandos" is on canvas.

Canvas was coming into use in England in the early 1600s, but I believe its use for portraits was not at all common until the later Jacobean period. And as Cooper herself observes in the catalogue, a "feigned oval" as early as 1610 "would have been a relatively new format", despite its deployment in the far more splendid 1595 portrait (on panel) of John Donne.

She ignores my suggestion that "Chandos" could be a copy made from an *ad vivum* original for Burbage's King's Men successor Joseph Taylor in 1619/20, being acquired by Davenant after Taylor's death in 1652. The dates fit. This theory also has the merit of accommodating the testimonies of Vertue and Oldys.

Katherine Duncan-Jones

JUNE 16, 2006

I too have viewed the Searching for Shakespeare exhibition. Amid all the focus on alleged portraits of Shakespeare, however, there was no mention made of an important early witness to Shakespeare's image. This is the sketch of Shakespeare's original monument in Holy Trinity Church, Stratford-upon-Avon, made by the antiquary William Dugdale in 1634.

It has long been known that the existing Shakespeare monument at Stratford was restored in the eighteenth century. Less known is that evidence of the original monument exists. Dugdale's drawing shows a figure, not holding a pen and paper (a later interpolation), but resting both hands upon a cushion or woolsack. Far from being that of a self-satisfied butcher, the face looks gaunt and austere, with a long, drooping moustache.

Next to that engraving, the Dugdale drawing offers us the earliest undisputed and independent evidence of how Shakespeare might have looked.

Peter Beal

JUNE 23, 2006

Peter Beal is hardly ever wrong, but there is a dangerous slip in his letter about Dugdale's sketch. He does not reflect what Diana Price wrote in her 1997 article on the matter. The pen is not "a later interpolation": it was a removable accessory, as on other funeral monuments of writers, which over the years has been taken by souvenir-hunters. The cushion, though, is not a woolsack: it clearly has tassels on each of its four corners. Who ever heard of a tasselled woolsack?

The most accurate image of Shakespeare's monument prior to its restoration in 1749 is in fact the sketch made by George Vertue, now in the British Library, where pen and cushion are clearly visible.

Why does any of this matter? Because the absence of a pen in Dugdale and the "woolsack" canard have been used by anti-Stratfordians as supposed evidence that the Stratford man was a wool-dealer rather than a dramatist and that someone else wrote the plays (though they struggle to explain why a wool-dealer's monument would have an epitaph making comparisons to Socrates and Virgil, to "all he hath writt" and to the "living art" he has left behind).

Jonathan Bate

JUNE 30, 2006

I'm afraid that Jonathan Bate, setting out to correct Peter Beal, himself falls into error. The Dugdale sketch does indeed show the subject resting both hands upon a woolsack or woolpack, which the *OED* defines as "a great number of Fleeces made up together in a cloth tied at the four ends". The four knots (not tassels) are made by tying small stones into the corners with string, so creating "ears", which were easier to grasp when lifting the sacks.

When Nicholas Rowe produced the first newly edited Works of Shakespeare in 1709 he commissioned a new version of Dugdale's engraving, hands on woolsack, with the fingers of the right hand certainly not "disposed as if holding a pen", as Sidney Lee claimed in 1908.

The first sketch to show the subject of this monument holding a pen and a piece of paper (the hands still resting, absurdly enough, on a woolsack or

cushion) was made by George Vertue in 1723 for Pope's Shakespeare, and was evidently based on the Chandos portrait. The position of the face, elbows and hands is quite different from those in the monument as we know it today, which may date from the extensive restorations carried out by Joseph Greene in 1749.

The scholar Richard Kennedy, who first identified John Ford as author of the "Funerall Elegye", has put all these facts together and drawn the conclusion that the original monument represented Shakespeare's father, John, a "considerable dealer in wool."

A monument to his memory would not have been out of place in the local church. Dugdale recorded two other monuments in Holy Trinity to woolmen.

Bate is worried that the anti-Stratfordians may seize on this evidence to deny that Shakespeare was the most famous dramatist of his generation. I would be more worried that, by distorting the evidence, we might perpetuate the myths attached to his biography.

Brian Vickers

 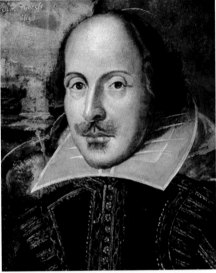 

JULY 7, 2006

Brian Vickers is hardly ever wrong, but he too has been misled by the "woolsack" myth. The 1623 First Folio includes a poem by Leonard Digges, step-son of Thomas Russell (a Stratford man who oversaw the signing of Shakespeare's will), referring to the "Stratford monument" of "the deceased author Master William Shakespeare". As I noted previously, the monument bears an inscription referring to the subject's writings and compares him to Socrates and Virgil – an unlikely accolade for Shakespeare's father. That inscription was there when Dugdale made his drawing. Whether or not the object in Dugdale's dodgy sketch resembles a knotted woolsack, the monument itself represents William Shakespeare with a quill and paper resting on a tasselled cushion, bolster or tablet. You can see it today, just as Leonard Digges saw it when it was new.

Jonathan Bate

JULY 7, 2006

Is it conceivable that the townspeople of Stratford, including the dramatist's widow, his two daughters, his son-in-law, and the church authorities, all of whom knew what Shakespeare looked like, permitted the erection of a monument depicting John Shakespeare to be inscribed with verses in English and Latin that clearly refer to his son? Moreover, Professors Bate and Vickers ignore the crucial point that there is no reason to believe that the appearance of the figure on the monument was materially different in 1634 from what it is now. At the time the monument was restored, in or around 1748, Joseph Greene wrote that great pains were taken to preserve its integrity.

Stanley Wells

JULY 14, 2006

The article by Richard J. Kennedy, to which Brian Vickers refers and which Professor Bate unfairly dismisses as "shoddy", leaves no doubt that the hands in the Dugdale drawing are pressing into a woolsack. In the present monument, this object has become some kind of "cushion, bolster or tablet", as Bate notes – a curiously unsuitable writing surface for the poet now represented with pen in hand, and perhaps more akin to a prie-dieu.

In any case, these features could hardly be mistaken for one another. Neither could the positioning of the arms and hands, the shape of the head, or the moustache (long and drooping in the drawing, short and upturned in the present monument). These differences are too great to be dismissed simply as "dodgy" drawing on Dugdale's part.

When publishers of the period boast of the accuracy and authenticity of their editions, scholars often view such claims with scepticism. Yet Professor Wells expects us to accept literally the rather fulsome account by the antiquary Joseph Greene.

While it is clear that the monument drawn by Dugdale, was accepted in his day as being that of Shakespeare, mysteries still persist. Why are certain features of the monument more befitting the profession and civic status of the playwright's father? This and other questions raised by the Dugdale drawing can only be answered if it is taken seriously by scholars and not consigned indignantly to the waste bin because it does not tally with cherished conceptions.

Peter Beal

Pillow talk

In September 2014 a *TLS* book review referred to the 'primarily homosexual context' of Shakespeare's Sonnets. In a letter the following week, Professor Brian Vickers, said it was 'anachronistic' to suggest that the Sonnets could not be, in part, about male friendship. Other letters followed and the story soon caught the attention of the tabloids – *The Sun*'s headline was 'Romeo meets Julian'

OCTOBER 3, 2014

Jason Scott-Warren states that Shakespeare's Sonnet 116 occurs in a "primarily homosexual context", but this anachronistic assumption needs to be questioned. True, the first seventeen poems in this collection are addressed to a young man urging him to marry and beget children in order to pass on his beauty to posterity, but Shakespeare derived that speech situation, and many of his arguments, from Erasmus's "Encomium Matrimonii", a model epistle translated in Thomas Wilson's *Arte of Rhetorique* (1560). Such a concern may be an expression of friendship but it is hardly a recognized homosexual position for the time.

That said, the unique feature of Shakespeare's sonnets compared to other Renaissance collections is the absence of a named female addressee. Here is no Laura, no Stella, Hélène, Cassandre, Delia, Geraldine, or a dozen more, whose "cruelty" is a theme to be deplored in a thousand variations. And whereas those unpersuadable mistresses are mostly referred to in the third person, the other remarkable feature of Shakespeare's collection is its person-to-person address. I count just over a hundred instances of the third-person pronoun "he" or "she",

compared to about 960 of the first person ("I", "me", "my", "mine") and 890 instances of the second person ("thou", "thee", "thy", "thine", together with fewer instances of "you" forms, often chosen for euphony – try saying "thinkst thou that they threaten"). These are, to an unprecedented degree, "I" and "thou" poems, which are therefore gender-neutral. They map phases of relationships which any reader can pass through, including fulfilment, betrayal, consolation. This undefined, unconstrained speech situation is the reason why they are universally applicable, in a way that sonnets addressed to Laura or Stella, however poetically distinguished, can never be. In experiencing these poems, every reader is an "I" or "thou", whatever their sex.

Brian Vickers

OCTOBER 31, 2014

Brian Vickers makes an interesting point about the "unnamedness" of the poet's lover(s) or friend(s) – and one might add his rival poet(s) in Sonnets nos 78–86 – and revives a well-known observation about the affinity of Sonnets 1–17 with an epistle in Erasmus's "Encomium Matrimonii" and its translation by Thomas Wilson

(1553, not 1560). But not for the first time in the *TLS* does Sir Brian introduce as critical or biographical *données* presuppositions that many of us would question, if not reject out of hand. That Sonnet 116 appears in "a primarily homosexual context" may be an overstatement, and that the "marry and breed" sequence (nos 1–17) expresses "male friendship but excludes sodomy" is at least arguable, but the sexual ambivalence of the 1609 volume is hardly a matter for debate any more – nor is the notion of bisexuality or homosexuality "anachronistic" for Elizabethan poets and playwrights (Marlowe, Beaumont and Fletcher, et al).

As early as 1640 the editor of Shakespeare's poems omitted passages and altered pronouns to conceal homoerotic implications, and the comparative neglect of the 1609 canon in its entirety for nearly 200 years cannot be unrelated to the same moralistic concerns. I cannot think of any responsible editor or critic of the Sonnets in our own day who would dismiss the premise of homosexual – as well as heterosexual – passion pervading the sequence. Shakespeare does not seem embarrassed to lay bare his feelings towards his male comrade/patron/lover: the uneasiness is all ours.

A more insidious but fashionable *donnée*, and to my mind one of the great fallacies of modern Shakespeare criticism, is that the poet addresses his sonnet-subjects just as if he were composing dialogue for characters in his plays, for "autobiographical interpretations [of the sonnet texts] are fictive". We can trace this presumption to the nineteenth-century biographical wars that Samuel Schoenbaum has chronicled, probably commencing as a response to extrapolations from dramatic passages, but as applied nowadays to a non-dramatic text it seems almost uniquely Shakespearean, and unjustifiably so. For literary context, however you slice it, cannot be ignored: sonnets are not plays, and first-person lyric poets rarely if ever adopt a deceptive "persona" in order to feign feelings they do not experience. Of course, much elegiac and amatory verse of the period is formulaic, but most sonnets and personally circulated lyrics are usually regarded as the last refuge of sincerity. We do not question Petrarch's infatuation with his "Laura" any more than we distrust Keats's devotion to Fanny Brawne: why should Shakespeare alone be thought so committed to the "negative capability" of his dramatic craft that all his most personal writings are treated as potentially artificial?

Arthur Freeman

NOVEMBER 7, 2014

I am not a Shakespearean scholar, and would make no pronouncements about what may or may not underlie the content of his Sonnets. But the Italian actress Isabella Andreini published her own *Rime* in 1601. Her opening sonnet makes it clear that the reader is not to take the amorous vicissitudes explored in parts of the collection as applying to her. Rather, she says, she is using her artistic virtuosity to describe fictional passions. She was keen to disassociate herself from non-respectable emotions and liaisons; to show that a professional actress could also be a virtuous wife and mother.

Shakespeare may not have been doing this at all; but we must note that during his lifetime it was possible for another author to offer lyric poems as fiction – "sonnets as plays" in Mr Freeman's terms.

Richard Andrews

NOVEMBER 14, 2014

Arthur Freeman objects to my remark that "autobiographical interpretations [of the sonnet texts] are fictive". I could have added that they are also a waste of time, since nothing can be established about "Mr WH", the Dark Lady or "The Rival Poet". Everyone should consult the magnificent two-volume edition by Hyder Rollins (1944) for his dry wit documenting the extent of human folly. Mr Freeman backs up his interpretation with a general, apodictic statement, that "first-person lyric poets rarely if ever adopt a deceptive 'persona' in order to feign feelings they do not experience". But many would object that they do so all the time! Shakespeare may have experienced many things, but he was capable of imagining many more.

Mr Freeman argues that the "neglect" of the Sonnets for 200 years must have been related to "moralistic concerns", but the form hardly outlived the Renaissance, with Milton its last great exponent. This was the reason for their neglect, not the peculiarly modern cycle Mr Freeman constructs of shame, guilt, suppression and scandal.

Brian Vickers

NOVEMBER 21, 2014

Brian Vickers's remark that "autobiographical interpretations are fictive" and "a waste of time" because they cannot hope to identify persons

to whom some of the poems are addressed, ignores the fact that such interpretations may tell us something about their author. When a poet whose name is William writes poems of anguished and unabashed sexual frankness which pun on the word "will" – thirteen times in No 135 – and which include one (136) which ends with the words "my name is Will", it is not unreasonable to conclude that he may be writing from the depths of his own experience.

Vickers's remark that the sonnet form "hardly outlived the Renaissance, with Milton as its last great exponent", suggests that he has never heard of Wordsworth, Keats, Christina Rossetti, Gerard Manley Hopkins, Thom Gunn, and all the other poets who since Milton's time have used the form to express deeply personal and, often, clearly autobiographical concerns.

Stanley Wells

NOVEMBER 21, 2014

Richard Andrews's answer to Arthur Freeman citing the sonnets of Isabella Andreini makes an interesting claim, though here may be a case of a lady protesting too much. As for Petrarch, he himself maintained the existence of Laura, which rather supports Freeman's case for biographical relevance.

It is tempting to see Shakespeare's Sonnets as pure fiction, but that only partly explains the existence and function of a half-realized figure such as the "rival poet". As for the so-called Dark Lady, nowhere in his theatre does Shakespeare end, as he does Sonnet 152, in condemning a woman quite so vituperatively, without conceding at least something to her, if only a dimension of pathos. His motives for holding out on her, with an uncharacteristic lack of generosity, continue to puzzle, and would seem to smack of unresolved personal business.

John Roe

ESSAYS

Idle worship

Those who seek to deny Shakespeare's authorship of more than thirty plays, two narrative poems and a collection of sonnets are driven to strange expedients. Consider the following stories:

AUTHOR: BRIAN VICKERS

Francis Bacon, despite his busy life as a barrister, involved in both state and private legal cases, who kept up his connections with Gray's Inn as a law lecturer, an MP and chairman of several committees, a rising government legal officer, and a scholar whose avowed ambition was to reform science so that it could benefit mankind, despite all this, had enough time to write the works published under Shakespeare's name, with the connivance of the actor from Stratford. Either they managed to deceive all the theatre people with whom Shakespeare worked on a daily basis – his fellow actors; those who shared with him the management of both the theatre company (the Lord Chamberlain's Men until 1603, thereafter the King's Men) and their playhouse (the Theatre until 1599, thereafter the Globe); and the playwrights (Peele, Middleton, Wilkins, Fletcher) with whom he co-authored at least six plays – or else all these people were in on the secret. Bacon concealed his authorship during his and Shakespeare's lifetime, but thoughtfully left some encoded messages in the First Folio, which were not deciphered until 1856. Bacon was also the President or Imperator of the Rosicrucians, an adept of the Kabbalah, and the leading English freemason.

Although Christopher Marlowe was to all appearances killed in a tavern brawl in Deptford on May 30, 1593, his death being certified at an inquest held on June 1 and presided over by the Queen's coroner, at which sixteen local jurors acquitted the assailant, Ingram Frazer, on the grounds of self-defence, this was all an elaborate scam arranged by Thomas Walsingham, Queen Elizabeth's spymaster and Marlowe's homosexual lover. The body buried in an unmarked grave in St Nicholas's Churchyard on June 1 was in fact that of John Penry, the Separatist leader, who had just been executed. With the help of the Muscovy Company, Marlowe was spirited away to Scotland, or Russia, or Italy, whence he entered into "the Shakespeare Compact", an agreement under which his works appeared

RIGHT
Eminent scholars have roundly debunked the arguments of those who purport that Francis Bacon, pictured, wrote Shakespeare's plays

under that actor's name, including co-authored ones, subject to the difficulties previously mentioned. The true story, not revealed until 1955, persuaded those who erected a plaque to Marlowe in Westminster Abbey to give his death date as "1593?".

The genesis of such theories is to be found in the Shakespeare idolatry expressed by so many nineteenth-century commentators, which produced a counter-reaction summed up in the book by RM Theobald (Hon Sec of the Bacon Society), *Dethroning Shakespeare* (1888). Avid bardolators had ascribed to him a remarkable knowledge of Greek, Latin and other languages; wide reading; expert knowledge of the law; a huge vocabulary, introducing many new words into English, and so on. The Baconians objected that virtually nothing was known of Shakespeare's life, that he was illiterate, a mere actor and a plagiarist. By contrast, Bacon was skilled in several languages, an eminent lawyer, a man of vast intellect, and so a rival idolatry was set up.

The Baconian enthusiasts conveyed their theories in huge volumes, 675 pages for Delia Bacon's *The Philosophy of the Plays of Shakespeare Unfolded* (1857), 1,000 pages for Ignatius Donnelly's *The Great Cryptogram: Francis Bacon's Cipher in the So-called Shakespeare Plays* (1888). The excitement of toppling the idol released huge quantities of psychic confidence, encouraging Donnelly to ascribe to Bacon the authorship of Montaigne's *Essays*, Burton's *Anatomy of Melancholy* and the plays of Marlowe and at least seven other dramatists. Sir Edward Durning-Lawrence in *Bacon Is Shakespeare* (1910) also credited Bacon with the *Authorized Version of the Bible*, and believed that Bacon had written Montaigne's essays in the original French.

None of the Baconians was a literary scholar, none of them felt the need to acquire any knowledge of English literature, or the English language in the sixteenth century, and none bothered to read Bacon, although the magnificent fourteen-volume edition of James Spedding was completed in 1874. All they needed was the preconceived notion that Shakespeare could not have written the plays, while Bacon could. A semblance of expertise was provided by lawyers and judges ready to pronounce that the plays demonstrated a knowledge of the law only possible to a trained lawyer. Unfortunately, these lawyers had no knowledge of Elizabethan literature, and did not realize that the works of many other dramatists – Lyly, Greene, Chapman, Jonson, Dekker, Heywood, Massinger – contain extended passages of legal jargon in comparison to which those in the Shakespeare plays seem like fleeting allusions. These oversights were documented in great detail by JM Robertson in *The Baconian Heresy: a Confutation* (1913), still the best study of this delusion, who devoted nearly 200 pages to demonstrating that legalisms pervaded Elizabethan and Jacobean literature.

The Baconian case uses a kind of literary "identikit", deducing from Shakespeare's plays a series of capabilities that the actor from Stratford could not have possessed, but exaggerating them in the process, until they reach unreal dimensions. As Robertson pointed out, they were unwittingly aided by "idolatrous Shakespeareans (who) set up a visionary figure of the Master", so playing into the Baconians' hands. In *The Classical Allusions in the Shakespeare Plays* (1908), RM Theobald claimed to find traces of a hundred Greek and Latin authors, some of them extremely obscure (Anaxandrides, Artemidorus, Arianus, Avienus…). The briefest examination shows that Theobald's learning was misplaced, for to cite Laurentius Abstemius as the source of the phrase "wolf in sheep's array" or Athenaeus for "bull-bearing Milo" is to demonstrate your ignorance of all the other more likely sources on which Shakespeare could have drawn.

Robertson devoted another 200 pages to an exposure of this fallacy, also demolishing the anti-Stratfordians' claim that the plays contained such a huge vocabulary and word-creation that the actor from Stratford could never have written them. Robertson showed that the size of Shakespeare's vocabulary was not exceptional, and that the *Oxford English Dictionary* gave earlier dates for the 200-odd words claimed as occurring for the first time in the plays. None of the Baconians had bothered to study Bacon's vocabulary, but Robertson showed how different it was from Shakespeare's. His refutation is never cited by the Baconians, who know where to draw a veil.

Robertson had no illusion that he had silenced the Baconians. Many of their current claims had been made years before, he noted, "but they seem to recur spontaneously", and he added, "if I can forecast the future with any safety from my knowledge of the Baconian movement, the common run of Baconians will go on as before".

Peter Dawkins's book *The Shakespeare Enigma* (2004) proved Robertson's point: it is a digest of all the anti-Stratfordians' clichés and errors. "The facts we have about Shakespeare's literary life … are outstandingly few. Indeed, one could say that they are virtually nil." Well, it is true that some Elizabethans have almost disappeared from view. What we know of the literary career of that great writer Thomas Kyd can be written on the back of an envelope. For Richard Hathway, described by Francis Meres as among the "best for comedy", *Henslowe's Diary* records the titles of eighteen plays he co-authored for the Admiral's and Worcester's Men between 1598 and 1603: none has survived. For Shakespeare, by contrast, we have a large number of Quarto editions, produced by many different publishers, on the title-pages of which his name occurs more often than that of any other dramatist of the period, together with two narrative poems personally dedicated to his patron Southampton. We have a huge number of allusions, both laudatory and envious, from fellow writers and others in the London theatre world who knew him well (Greene, Meres, Jonson, Heywood, Webster, Marston, Gabriel Harvey, Chettle, Weever, Dekker); an almost continuous series of references from 1592 to his death in 1616, all of which identify him as both actor and author. Many legal documents have survived, and of the available biographical sources it is enough to mention two: Samuel Schoenbaum's *William Shakespeare: a Documentary Life* (1975), and the more inclusive collection by Catherine Loomis, *William Shakespeare, The Life Records, volume 263* in Gale's *Dictionary of Literary Biography* (2002). This runs to more than 300 pages, including facsimiles and transcripts of all documents connected with Shakespeare and his family, all records of the theatrical companies with which he was involved, and all significant allusions up to 1612. Dawkins simply recycles the stock-in-trade of the anti-Stratfordians since the nineteenth century, that there are no records of Shakespeare possessing books – but nor are there for Bacon.

There are many odd things in *The Shakespeare Enigma*, but one of the oddest is the laudatory foreword by Mark Rylance, then artistic director of the New Globe Theatre and chairman of the Shakespeare Authorship Trust, in which he repeats some of the anti-Stratfordians' oldest errors ("the actor Shakespeare's extremely limited access to learning"..."so little known as a writer in his own life"). Rylance professes to be an "agnostic" on this

Denial of Shakespeare follows exactly the same FLAWED reasoning as HOLOCAUST denial

SCOTT MCCREA

issue, and "welcomes all forms of interest in Shakespeare", even that which denies his authorship of the plays. It is reasonable to be agnostic about the existence of God, but not about a dramatist who left so many proofs, direct and indirect, of his "right happy and copious industry", as Webster described it.

The success of the New Globe as an acting space, under Rylance's direction, is a tribute to all the scholars who have reconstructed Elizabethan theatre architecture. The same scholarly methods have established beyond doubt Shakespeare's authorship (and co-authorship) of his plays, so one can hardly lick one hand and bite the other.

Bacon may be the oldest authorship candidate, but there are others. The case for Edward de Vere (1550-1604) was first made by Thomas J Looney, in *"Shakespeare" Identified* (1920). Looney constructed his own identikit of the general features possessed by the author of Shakespeare's works, with the usual demand that he be "of superior education – classical", and some special provisos, "a man with feudal connections", "a member of the higher aristocracy". This mixture of snobbery and ignorance as to the nature of Elizabethan grammar school education eliminated Shakespeare but identified the seventeenth Earl of Oxford, a courtier poet with some twenty fairly conventional lyrics to his name. There are several insuperable objections to Oxford's candidature: he died with a dozen of Shakespeare's sole and co-authored plays unwritten (or at least unperformed); the style of his poetic oeuvre is extremely limited; he led a wasteful aristocratic existence, abroad and at home. Looney tried to get round the first difficulty by re-dating the plays, and in the years since he wrote the Oxfordians have

invented a new chronology, improbably dating Shakespeare's early comedies to the late 1570s, and postulating that Oxford left drafts of all the remaining plays for Shakespeare to touch up and pass off as his own, either completely hoaxing everyone connected with the Globe, or relying on their connivance.

The Oxfordian cause has been pursued with the perverse enthusiasm that any anti-Stratfordian candidate generates: a curious psychological phenomenon. Supporters may sustain themselves with the sense of cocking a snook at official culture, or exposing an evil conspiracy whose existence was unsuspected for 300 years. Certainly, metaphors of detection and exposure abound, as in the title of one of the Oxfordians' sacred texts, Charlton Ogburn's *The Mysterious William Shakespeare: the Myth and the Reality* (1984). But whatever the Oxfordians are producing, it is not scholarship.

In *The Case for Shakespeare*, Scott McCrea suggests that "denial of Shakespeare follows exactly the same flawed reasoning as Holocaust denial" in that it rejects the most obvious explanation of an event, and reinterprets evidence to fit a preconceived idea ("the ovens at Auschwitz baked bread"). Facts that contradict the theory are explained by conspiracy, but this ploy means that "conspiracy theories are really not theories at all", but faiths, which cannot be proved false.

As we survey the never-ending flow of anti-Shakespeare books it is hard not to share the bitterness of Georg Brandes, moved in part to write his *William Shakespeare* (1898) by the "ignorant and arrogant attack" of the "wretched group of dilettanti" who have "been bold enough ... to deny William Shakespeare the right to his own life-work". ∎

Miscell

anies

ESSAYS

Greasepaint and oils

There's scant record of Shakespeare having inspired artists while he was alive but, as an exhibition at Dulwich Picture Gallery showed, the stage became a popular subject for painters

AUTHOR: NICHOLAS ROBINS

Shakespeare is not known for his interest in artists. There is the solitary reference to "that rare Italian master Giulio Romano" in *The Winter's Tale*, probably derived from the epitaph as it appears in Vasari, which boasts of the painter's ability to make "sculpted and painted bodies breathe". And even that, of course, is a bit of a joke, since Giulio was never a sculptor, and Hermione, still breathing, never a sculpture. Can Shakespeare have borne a grudge against painters? He was always aware of the visual possibilities of the theatre; his visual imagination is incomparable and his interest in artistic practice forms part of his way of describing the difference between appearance and reality.

The sorrows of Richard II make the King see the world in the manner of one trying to make out the skull in Holbein's "Ambassadors":

Like perspectives, which rightly gazed upon
Show nothing but confusion – eyed awry,
Distinguish form.

But, unless the Great Fire or some other holocaust has swept away a taproom or two decorated with Hamlet in the graveyard or an apotheosis of Falstaff throwing out a plump calf and dashing down a mug of sack on the ceiling of a backroom bar in Eastcheap, the painter-stainers seem never to have returned the compliment. Henry Peacham's wretchedly ambiguous sketch of *Titus Andronicus*, as anyone at all familiar with the early performance of Shakespeare's plays will know, is the only image we have. Even the one surviving representation of the interior of a public playhouse – the almost equally ambiguous Swan – casts only the most oblique light on "Shakespeare". It is, by any standards, a feeble visual legacy.

The absence of a visual yardstick with which to beat the genius of succeeding generations into a sixteenth-century party line has, of course, proved liberating. And for the past 300 or so years, painters have been trying to make good their

RIGHT
'The Death of Ophelia', by Eugène Delacroix, 1858. Delacroix chose subjects from Shakespeare's plays – *Hamlet*, in particular – several times

oversight – from the Sicilian landscape which is the real subject of Francesco Zuccarelli's "Macbeth, Banquo and the Witches", to the minute stage directions discernible in Holman Hunt's "Valentine Rescuing Silvia from Proteus", that agonizing moment of shame and betrayal towards the end of *The Two Gentlemen of Verona* – a painting which could have been based on a performance produced by Ruskin and directed by George Eliot. Hogarth, for his part, depicted a lovely scene from *The Tempest*, with its layered pyramidal composition and – sometimes overlooked in Hogarth – exquisite painterliness. It seems more of an English commentary on the High Renaissance Venetian style, for, with Prospero as an intermediary between the votary Ferdinand and the Madonna-like Miranda, Hogarth has given us a Shakespearean *conversazione*. His earlier "Falstaff examining his Troops" might have had the actor John Harper's Falstaff as its starting point, but this is surely as much an imaginary as a

historical performance. And Hogarth's chief interests, in any case, lie elsewhere: notably in the accumulation of decor which comments on and subverts the main narrative.

Then there is Johann Zoffany's portrait of "Macklin as Shylock" (c. 1768), which shows him in a studio, not as he ever appeared on a stage, a decontextualized Macklin-as-Shylock, a Shylock in essence. He is, in fact, a character who might exist somewhere outside the bounds of the play, raging away in some balconied interior and living a life outside his lines. Zoffany shows us a character and situation condensed, rather in the manner of one of those unhistorical conflations which appear in late-medieval art, a *pietà* or an *ecce homo*: not the depiction of a moment but an object of reverie, waiting for that bewildering rush of Victorian speculation on the personal history of Shakespeare's characters. Only six years after this picture appeared, Maurice Morgann published his incomparable character study of Falstaff, who "passes thro' the Play as a lawless meteor, and we wish to know what course he is afterwards likely to take".

Few artists seem to have made the comparison between the tasks of the actor and the artist. Delacroix did, and rather misleadingly: "Execution in painting must always have an element of improvisation in it, and it is chiefly in this that it differs from that of the actor". It seems an oddly blinkered distinction. One of Shakespeare's most static, pictorial passages inspired Delacroix's "Death of Ophelia", although the figure itself is probably derived from Poussin's "Echo and Narcissus". Indeed, it seems as much an improvisation on Poussin as it is on Shakespeare: Narcissus's arm has been awkwardly modified in order to keep hold of the coronet of weeds Ophelia was trying to hang on

ABOVE
'Macklin as Shylock',
Johann Zoffany,
c. 1768

the "envious sliver", and the vivid picture Gertrude (and Millais) gives of her singing "incapable of her own distress" is softened into that generalized enchantment Delacroix found in the play. "After Shakespeare", wrote Baudelaire, "no one has excelled like Delacroix in fusing a mysterious unity of drama and reverie." His last (1859) and weakest rendition of Hamlet in the graveyard is also here. The composition comes off and the colouring is lovely, but there is something vague and lumpish about Hamlet and Horatio.

Opportunities to demonstrate the nineteenth century's three-way transaction between art, theatre and history are best provided by *Henry VIII*, into whose spectacular reign the scenic designers could wander about and snap up whatever they liked. In George Harlow's "Trial of Queen

Katherine" (1817), the reality of the drama is not what it presents but what is represented within it, the history behind the play, which it endeavours to reanimate. Nathaniel Dance's portrait of "David Garrick as Richard III", his wardrobe at Bosworth Field seemingly supplied by a partnership of Lord Burleigh and George III, had suggested that in 1771 Shakespeare was still the poet of nature, whose general truths need never be restricted to one period.

For the Kembles and their successors, as Harlow and others here show, Shakespeare was the poet of history, on whose behalf the past's material legacy must be scrupulously retrieved. The plays become a kind of telescope through which we might discern the actual, the historical reality. Charles Kemble's Henry VIII of 1831 was, according to the Theatrical Observer, "so well dressed and so well stuffed that if Holbein's picture of bluff King Hal could walk out of its frame and speak, we question if it would present us with a more perfect portrait". All Is True, then.

Lastly, in the context of the Kemble era, a dynasty characterized by Hazlitt as the "still life and statuary of the stage", Henry Fuseli's "Lady Macbeth Seizing the Daggers" of 1812 seems all the more extraordinary. In his youth, Fuseli had seen Garrick and Pritchard perform the Macbeth depicted here by Zoffany in his double portrait of the pair wearing eighteenth-century dress in front of a gothic backdrop. Fuseli's is a theatre of imagination and memory, and Desmond Shawe-Taylor has argued that the image represents the Macbeths in some circle of Dante's Inferno, condemned to rehearse their crime for ever. They are already dead Lady Macbeth seems a membrane of smoke, her husband, with his flayed Francis Bacon-like midriff, to have leapt from an anatomy book: a ghost from Vesalius. ∎

Something rocking in Denmark

A Shakespeare Music Catalogue lists over 20,000 musical compositions that have been written in aid and honour of Shakespeare, and the many artistic projects inspired by him

AUTHOR: BRIAN VICKERS

For nearly four centuries now, composers have turned Shakespeare's plays and poems, poetry and prose, into music. Many (perhaps the majority) have composed on commission from a theatrical company, and some have written to order for a specific anniversary or public celebration. But others, hundreds of them, have been moved by a particular play, character, or song, to write music out of themselves, an individual response translating one artistic medium into another. The index to *A Shakespeare Music Catalogue* runs together composers and arrangers, but for *As You Like It* alone I count over a thousand different composers who have written music for all or part of the play.

This is a unique cultural phenomenon (no other writer is remotely comparable) and of apparently universal distribution. *A Shakespeare Music Catalogue* – the work of two main editors and one associate, incorporating material

collected over forty years by the American musicologist Charles Haywood, and listing a team of eleven research assistants – lists more than 20,000 compositions in its bibliography, for instance. Under Mendelssohn, we find accounts of how his *Midsummer Night's Dream* music was banned by the Nazis, and replaced by the acceptably Aryan compositions of Wager-Régeny, Weismann, Wolpert, and Zilcher (all of whom can be found in the main catalogue, but without indication of the circumstances in which they achieved such fame). There is a great number of professional Shakespeare composers who produce to order, year in year out, music for *Titus Andronicus, Cymbeline, Coriolanus*, or whatever is on the season's programme. Contemporary theatre companies are to be congratulated for their enlightened attitude to music. The Royal Shakespeare Company maintains a permanent music staff of fifteen, including an orchestra of ten, trains actors to sing, and is

BELOW
Adaptation of Shakespearean themes to popular musical forms has been going on since the seventeenth century

wholly committed to live performances, not pre-recorded tapes. No other company takes the music so seriously, but everywhere professionalism prevails. Yet these composers are in a rather odd position, creative artists who write music to fit not just a given text but also the director's "interpretation" of it in terms of the country or period in which he sets his production. For his Italianate *Much Ado* at the Old Vic in 1965, Frances Zeffirelli hired Nino Rota, the great master of pop film music. An RSC production of *The Two Gentlemen of Verona* was set by its director (David Thacker) in the 1930s, so Guy Woolfenden had to adapt his style to that idiom, becoming a Cole Porter here, a Purcell or Grieg next month. And so on this year and every year.

To many composers Shakespeare still represents a challenge which cannot be resisted. This no doubt derives in part from his status, since the late eighteenth century at least, as the supreme dramatist, or the world's greatest writer. But the incentive also derives from the role that music plays in his own work. The plays are full of allusions to music, as a symbol of cosmic and civic harmony, as eloquence, medicine, entertainment. There are many references to singing, to musical instruments and genres, to the technicalities of frets and sharps. His characters constantly quote snatches of songs, always adapted to the situation they find themselves in, yearning, mocking, regretting. Above all, the thirty or so songs he himself wrote positively demand musical setting, and composers have responded from their earliest years. Among Britten's unpublished juvenilia is a setting of "Take, o take those lips away" (*Measure for Measure*), dating from 1926, when he was thirteen. Walton recorded that he'd begun to write music when he was "about 12" (in 1914), with "settings of Shakespeare".

Shakespeare's challenge to the composer could be represented not just by a lyric but by a whole play. Writing to his brother Modest in May 1878, Pyotr Tchaikovsky outlined his plans for an opera on *Romeo and Juliet*, predicting that it "will he my very best work. It seems queer to me now that I did not realize long ago that I was chosen to write the music to this drama. I cannot imagine anything more appropriate to my musical talent". Tchaikovsky had already written his great "Fantasy Overture" for *Romeo and Juliet*, first in 1869 (revised in 1870 and again in 1880), but the opera itself never materialized, apart from sketches for a duet dating from about 1893.

Being possessed by Shakespeare is not an altogether happy state to be in. Robert Schumann, writing to his mother in December 1830,

described his plans for a "big opera; I am all on fire, and revel all day long in sweet fairy-like sounds. The opera is called 'Hamlet'; the thought of glory and immortality gives me strength and imagination." All that his creative fervour amounted to was a couple of pages of music notes headed "Sinfonia per il Hamlet".

Hamlet has attracted more unwritten music than any other text, the composers known to have projected operas including Glinka, Verdi, Mendelssohn, Debussy and Prokofiev. *Macbeth* attracted Chausson, Saint-Saëns, Wolf (who also had designs on *The Tempest*), and Hartmann, but to no avail. *The Tempest* produced schemes from Chabrier and Havergal Brian; *Timon of Athens* from Schoeck; and *Twelfth Night* from Johann Strauss. Some music-lovers contemplating these unwritten works may feel that the loss is not great, but one regrets that Wagner, having made two sketches for *Romeo and Juliet* in 1868, went no further.

The best-known unwritten Shakespeare opera is Verdi's *King Lear*, which he worked on between 1843 and 1857, with the librettists Cammarano and Somna: only two sketches survive (though Winton Dean has shown that the words of one of Cordelia's arias reappear in *Forza*). Verdi ultimately obtained a complete libretto, but claimed he had not found the right singers. The sheer massiveness of the text, rather than the composer's dilettantism, accounts for this opera's non-fruition. Pietro Mascagni had also planned an opera on *Lear*. Hearing of this, Verdi offered to pass on his own *Lear* material, which he had abandoned because "the scene when Lear is on the heath terrified

(him)". Mascagni, suitably discouraged that "the colossus of music-drama" had given up, dropped his scheme.

Adaptation to contemporary culture and to popular musical forms has been going on since the seventeenth century, at least, with the first "semi-operas", followed by the Shakespeare musicals mounted by Garrick with enormous success, and eliciting many happy and tuneful settings from Arne, Boyce, and JC Smith. The nineteenth century adapted Shakespeare to the grand opera traditions in the works of Bishop and Balfe. But it also produced a vigorous output of Shakespearean dance music. For the 1890 staging of *Antony and Cleopatra*, starring Lily Langtry, William Coni dedicated to her a waltz entitled "Queen of the Nile". *Cymbeline*, very popular with the Victorians, produced a "Cymbeline Valse", a "Cymbeline Mazurka", "Polka" and "March"; there was a "Hamlet Galop", an "Ophélie polka-mazurka" for military band, an "Ophelia polka" for solo zither, and a "Titania Galop" as a banjo solo.

Shakespeare was soon appropriated by jazz musicians. What one would give for a video recording of James Van Heusen's jazzed up *A Midsummer Night's Dream* (New York, 1939), called Swingin' the Dream, starring Louis Armstrong as Bottom and solo trumpet (could he play through the ass's head?), the Dandridge Sisters as the faeries, a Jitterbug Chorus, a Swing Choir, the Rhythmettes, three bands, and the Benny Goodman sextet (with Fletcher Henderson and Lionel Hampton!). Another performance by black actors in 1939 was a musical of *The Taming of the Shrew*, updated to Texas and New Orleans. There are scores by Max Roach and Duke Ellington, notably his *Such Sweet Thunder* (1957), a suite of twelve pieces including "Lady Mac", "The Telecasters" (depicting the Witches in *Macbeth* together with Iago), and "Sonnet to Hank Cinq". In Johnny Dankworth's *Shakespeare and All That Jazz* (1967), the text consists of "the titles of all the works in Shakespeare's canon". Since the 1960s there has been a veritable flood of rock operas and musicals, on every conceivable play. There are at least two rock operas on *Hamlet*: Gerry Pyle's *To Be* and Cliff Jones's *Kronborg: 1582*.

It is to be expected that most composers have chosen to set actual texts by Shakespeare. But one whole literary-musical genre arouses foreboding, the setting of famous speeches neither in a theatrical nor a musical context, but in a "commemorative" one, a situation which seems to slide fatally towards religiosity, patriotism or both. The patriotic texts are all too predictable, *Henry V* yielding such timely pieces as Rutland Boughton's "Agincourt" (1918), its libretto including words from an early English hymn, published in *The Motherland Song Book* (1919), or Frederick Bridge's setting of "O God of Battles" (subtitled "Shakespeare's Battle Prayer"), advertised in the *Musical Times* in April 1916 as "to be sung at Westminster Abbey. Royal Albert Hall. &c".

The religious uses to which Shakespeare has been put are at least less predictable. Few could have expected a German composer to produce König Lear: Eine keltische Passion (Wuppertal, 1956) by incorporating three Celtic hymns, or anticipated that a New Zealander, having written incidental music for *Measure for Measure*, should re-use it for a liturgical setting, punningly titled "Measured Mass" (Christchurch, 1978).

The incongruous is an area that Shakespeare music often gets into. Albert Tepper produced "A Portrait of Shylock" (New York, 1969) for, of all things, "a private Jewish wedding procession" – enough to blight any festivities, one might think. *The Merchant of Venice* was turned into a Xiang opera (Hunan, 1964), called "A Case of Human Flesh", a gruesome prospect. Sometimes the choice of resources seems bizarre: one Victorian composer writing music for *Antony and Cleopatra* introduces a song for a boys' choir; another gives Enobarbus a song called "The Sphinx". Modern composers seem especially prone to prescribing weird instruments, such as the metalophone and flexaphone (Berkeley, 1982), "three glass gongs, river stones, mortar and pestle, silver champagne goblets,

ABOVE
At the piano,
Duke Ellington,
whose album *Such
Sweet Thunder* was
a suite of twelve
Shakespeare-inspired
jazz pieces

music box interiors" (an Adelaide *As You Like It*, 1975), and a whole series of instruments designed by the composer for a Massachusetts performance of *Twelfth Night*, "Hand drs. Doblyria, sawblade, mrbm".

What is going on in the head of Debussy, meanwhile, when he writes "La Danse de Puck", or John Cage when he writes a piano piece called "Ophelia"? They are working from some "idea" of the character, however formed, and however translatable into musical terms. Composers can mysteriously transpose into purely musical forms not just individual characters but whole scenes, or even plays. For Beethoven there is the well-known anecdote of his reply to Schindler's request for "the key" to the piano sonatas Op 31, ii and Op 57 ("Appassionata"): "Just read Shakespeare's *Tempest*." Less well known, and more specific, is the story connected to his first string quartet, Op 18, i. After playing the second movement the composer asked Karl Amenda "what thought had been awakened by it"; Amenda replied, "it pictured for me the parting of two lovers". Beethoven's comment was "Good! I thought of the scene in the burial vault in *Romeo and Juliet*".

The obvious development inspired by Shakespeare is the tone poem. where composers often specify the incidents or characters that they have set to music. Richard Strauss had composed incidental music for *Romeo and Juliet* as early as 1887, aged twenty-three, and the original version of his tone poem *Macbeth* ended with a march celebrating the victory of Macduff, and he only revised it when it was pointed out that Shakespeare intended Macbeth, not Macduff, to be the hero of the play. ∎

All is but toys

Gather ingredients for the witches' pot and prepare for the siege
of Dunsinane Castle – we go back to the future to see what computer
games technology made of Shakespeare in 1986

AUTHOR: JULIA BRIGGS **ILLUSTRATION:** DARREN SMITH

Notoriously unlucky, *Macbeth* has the doubtful honour of being the first Shakespeare play to be turned into a computer game; the pursuit of goblins through Athenian woods and ghosts over Elsinore's battlements must soon follow. Oxford Digital Enterprises has produced four adventure games inspired by the play, interspersed with question-and-answer sessions that tackle the nitty-gritty of character and motivation, thus ballasting entertainment with education. A text of the play is also provided, with notes intended to reassure those who hold Shakespeare and his advocates in suspicion. The obvious target is the schoolchild, but the games are amusing and ingenious, while the knowledge of the play is at least as important as a knowledge of how computer adventure games work. Inevitably they illuminate some of the play's more forgettable moments along the way – you will need to know who Sweno was and what he was doing on St Colme's Inch. Odd bits of seventeenth-century folklore are dotted about among jokes as whiskery as any sporran, and if the games never attempt to capture the dark fatality of the original, they provide a lively quiz complete with sound and pictures.

The program begins with a thunderclap and an animated sequence of graphics to illustrate the first scene. Three black shapes shift continually in a bleak landscape until they finally resolve their formlessness into paddock, cat and owl. The player must now be Macbeth, and dispose first of a mounted gallowglass, then of Macdonwald, in suitably Shakespearean style. The graphics adjust in response to the correct instructions, and Macdonwald's head can be placed on the battlements, where it drips fitfully, if not fearfully. A number of rather less plausible actions must then be carried out if you are to reach the heath with Banquo and receive the witches' all-hail. Much lateral thinking is called for, and more patience, since a program written for a home computer is necessarily limited in vocabulary and syntax; the inventors of Macbeth have used nearly every byte of available memory in their effort to include as much Shakespearean vocabulary as possible, but the machine finds verbal richness and variety indigestible. Putting Shakespeare into computerspeak invites Johnson's comment, "It is not done well; but you are surprised to find it done at all."

Each game is drawn from a different section of the play; the third sets the player to collect the less gruesome ingredients of the witches' cauldron. This is played out against a sequence of different locations, with some of the objects needed forming part of the pictures themselves, as in old-fashioned puzzle books. Here yew berries must be picked in the moon's eclipse, root of hemlock dug for in the dark, and fenny snakes, owlets and newts retrieved from their habitats in various ways.

The second and fourth games are altogether more dramatic, since they are played against the clock, and their actions are rather more consonant with those of the play. For though the computer adventure partakes of the secret, mysterious and riddling nature of the witches as the proverbially open book cannot, the sinister atmosphere, the sense of nightmare and the ascendancy of darkness are not easily reproduced on the bright screen, amid joky asides. Yet these two games do suggest something of the hectic activity that flares up, to be succeeded with the play itself by horror or languor. In the second, the player as Lady Macbeth must find her way through the contrived corridors of Inverness Castle

to locate instructions and ingredients for the stirrup-cup to welcome Duncan, then feed him, drug the guards, and finally perform the murder, all within an hour. Creaking floorboards, a recalcitrant mandrake, Angus and Ross wandering at random about the castle, and Macbeth's last-minute hesitations all make the task more difficult. One feels the force of "'twere well it were done quickly." The last game finds Macbeth defending Dunsinane against the invaders, aided only by Seyton. After reading Dr Finlay's journal for Lady Macbeth's medical notes, hanging out banners, tossing a caber, and assembling the bagpipes to play "Auld Lang Syne" ("That was awful. You're out of practice", comments the computer) you may yet save yourself if your nerves are still sufficiently steady to type in the right instructions.

Similar home truisms turn up in the question-and-answer sessions that alternate with the games. Here a certain Sigmund F questions Macbeth and his lady in an attempt to define their nature and motives. Inevitably these interrogations smack of the old "how-many-children-had-Lady-Macbeth" chestnut, treating the characters as real people rather than walking shadows, poor puppets awaiting the decision of individual actors to animate them. At the same time they consistently direct attention to the play's central problems, several of which do lie in the nature of the inconsistencies they reveal. Ultimately the mechanical character of computer games cannot accommodate the organic genius of the play; but as a man of his time Shakespeare would at least have acknowledged the prescription of *dulce et utile* that underwrites this attempt. And Macbeth ranks as one of the most varied, inventive and original computer games yet written. ∎

This be the verse

In his 1925 review of George Coffin Taylor's book, *Shakespeare's Debt to Montaigne*, the poet notes that Shakespeare surely read with the most prodigious memory of words that has ever existed - helped by Montaigne's translator John Florio

AUTHOR: TS ELIOT

Mr Taylor confines himself, and rightly, to determining the extent of *verbal* influence [of John Florio's translation of Montaigne's *Essays on Shakespeare*]. His method is simple but persuasive. First he brings to light a number of fresh parallel passages of Florio's translation with passages in plays written after 1603 [when Florio's translation was published]. He does not rely on any one of the Shakespeare passages as obviously derived from Montaigne – though several of the parallels are to an unprejudiced mind quite convincing – but contends that the number of the parallels is sufficient to establish a strong probability that Shakespeare had the Florio Montaigne much in his mind, especially in the years immediately following 1603 – the later plays show fewer parallels. These parallels themselves are very interesting reading. But this mass of evidence is supported by evidence of another type, the presentation of which is Professor Taylor's most important contribution. Mr Taylor has compiled a list of words and phrases which are found in the Florio, and which were used by Shakespeare after Florio's book appeared and not before; words and phrases numbers enough to create a presumption that Shakespeare picked them up from Florio. Furthermore, Mr Taylor has drawn up a table showing the number of such words and phrases occurring in each play, and the percentage to each page: with the highly satisfactory result that (with two exceptions) the highest percentage is found in the plays written about or soon after 1603; from this date they decrease steadily, as, it would seem, the detailed impressions of the Florio faded from Shakespeare's mind. Of the two exceptions, Mr Taylor admits that "the strong influence in *The Tempest* is inexplicable, except on

the theory that Shakespeare retired for a brief interval to the reading of Montaigne." This hypothesis may look rather weak, but we think there is a great deal to be said for it. There is no doubt that *The Tempest* is a very late play, and it is the one play in which the influence of Montaigne is commonly acknowledged. As for *Othello*, in which the influence of Montaigne ought, on the theory, to be strong (the table shows a percentage of only 2.2 Montaigne words to the page, compared, for instance, with 2.8 in *The Winter's Tale*), we think that Mr Taylor should have expounded his explanation at greater length.

But, in any case, Mr Taylor attempts no more than to found a presumption; and in this we think he succeeds. As to the nature of the influence of Montaigne on Shakespeare he is wisely reserved. At most, a large part must be conceded to Florio himself – and here Mr Taylor renders a needed tribute to the work performed by the Elizabethan translators in enriching the language. Florio was compelled to draw upon every source of word-supply in our language and, when that supply was exhausted, to press into service foreign emissaries, words new and never spoken before in England. No one who will take the pains to read carefully two or three times through the Florio will doubt the vastness of the vocabulary. Let one cast about in one's mind for a source of available word-supply which could, about 1603, afford Shakespeare an opportunity for sudden expansion in vocabulary, and one will come at last to the Florio Montaigne.

Even, Mr Taylor adds, if we allow that Shakespeare may have got many of the words from other sources, such as the North Plutarch, or if Florio and Shakespeare were drawing on common sources, the evidence that Shakespeare

read with the most prodigious memory of words that has ever existed is almost indisputable, and is consonant with everything that we do know of Shakespeare. And in bringing to light this *verbal* influence Mr Taylor supplies a corrective to the invariable human impulse to look for mystery and excitement. For certainly it was not the influence of one philosopher on another. As Mr Taylor reminds us, no two critics can agree as to what Shakespeare's "philosophy" was – if he had one – and we need only recall such extreme limits of opinion as the views of Mr Santayana and Mr Middleton Murry. Montaigne is just the sort of writer to provide a stimulant to a poet; for what the poet looks for in his reading is not a philosophy – not a body of doctrine – but a point of departure. The attitude of the *craftsman* like Shakespeare – whose business was to write plays, not to think – is different from that of the philosopher or even the literary critic.

Not that Montaigne did not influence Shakespeare in ways which we can never know. Mr Taylor does not deny the existence of some deeper influence than an influence of vocabulary. But he refrains – and for this abstention must be given all praise – from attempting to plumb these depths. There was almost certainly some emotional influence. The characteristics of that mysterious and horrifying group of plays which includes *Hamlet* as well as *Measure for Measure* and *Troilus* must, we feel, owe something to Montaigne. But what and how much we shall never know. It is not only the external history of Shakespeare's life that is deficient. It is that internal history, which may have much or may have little relation to the external facts, that internal crisis over which our imagination is tempted to brood too long – it is this that we shall never know. ■

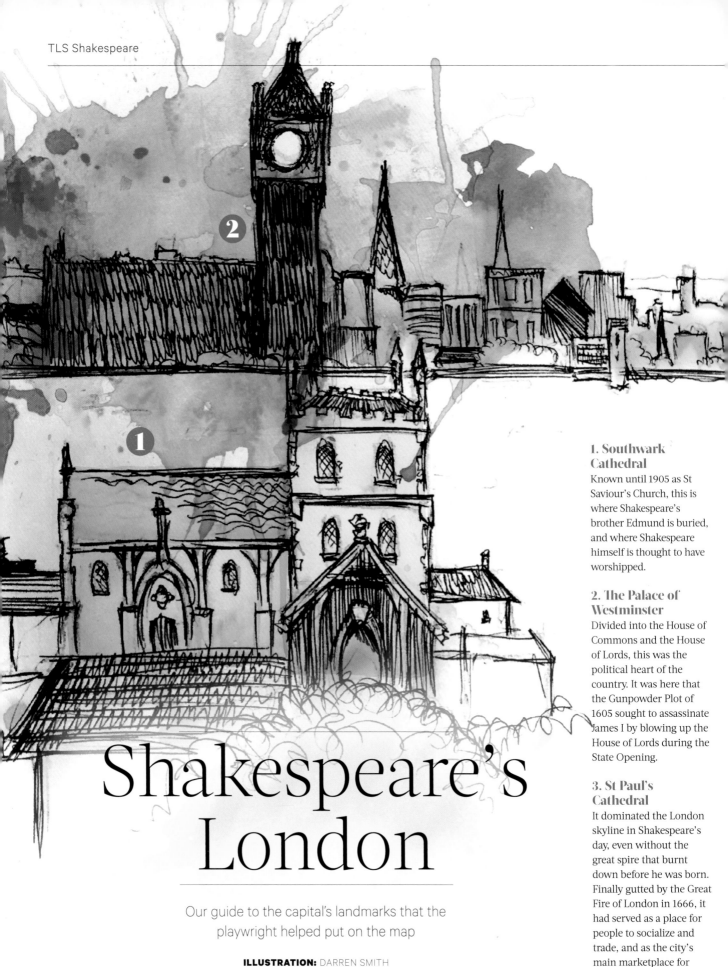

Shakespeare's London

Our guide to the capital's landmarks that the playwright helped put on the map

ILLUSTRATION: DARREN SMITH

1. Southwark Cathedral

Known until 1905 as St Saviour's Church, this is where Shakespeare's brother Edmund is buried, and where Shakespeare himself is thought to have worshipped.

2. The Palace of Westminster

Divided into the House of Commons and the House of Lords, this was the political heart of the country. It was here that the Gunpowder Plot of 1605 sought to assassinate James I by blowing up the House of Lords during the State Opening.

3. St Paul's Cathedral

It dominated the London skyline in Shakespeare's day, even without the great spire that burnt down before he was born. Finally gutted by the Great Fire of London in 1666, it had served as a place for people to socialize and trade, and as the city's main marketplace for

booksellers. In nearby London Wall, a block of stone with a medieval skull-and-crossbones carving marks another casualty of the fire: the spot where the graveyard of St Olave's church sat almost opposite the house in Silver Street where Shakespeare lodged for several years in the 1600s and wrote, among other works, *King Lear* and *Othello*.

4. The Tower of London

Formerly used as a royal residence, the Tower had become a prison by the sixteenth century, although not necessarily a terrible one: prisoners could purchase creature comforts from its commanding Lieutenant.

5. The River Thames

Enormously busy with both local traffic and the merchant ships that made London a major centre for English trade with the rest of the world, the river was also heavily polluted.

Throughout the seventeenth century, whenever it froze over, it became the site for a series of "frost fairs". Lined with houses and shops, London Bridge was the city's only bridge at this time. It wasn't demolished until the early nineteenth century.

6. The Globe

A theatre built in 1599 by Shakespeare's company, the Lord Chamberlain's Men, in Southwark, after a dispute over their previous venue in Shoreditch. It was burnt down in 1613, during a performance of *Henry VIII*, rebuilt in 1614, and then demolished in 1644. The modern Globe, which opened to the public in 1997, is based on the 1599 and 1614 buildings. The Rose theatre was already established on the south bank of the Thames when the Lord Chamberlain's Men built the Globe. Its remains can be seen today, beneath an office block, after being excavated in 1989.

DIALOGUES

Threepenny Lear

These two extracts from *The Messingkauf Dialogues,* a theoretical
work written by Bertolt Brecht in the 1930s and 1940s – and translated
by John Willett, who was *TLS* deputy editor in the 1960s – show the
playwright's admiration for Shakespeare's keen sense of time and place

LITERARY ADVISER: Shakespeare's plays are extraordinarily full of life. Apparently they were printed from the prompt copy, and took in all the changes made at rehearsal and the actors' improvisations. The way the blank verse is set down suggests that it must in many cases have been done by ear. *Hamlet* has always interested me specially. We know it was adapted from a previous play by a certain Thomas Kyd that had had a great success a few years earlier. Its theme is the cleansing of an Augean stable. The hero, Hamlet, cleans up his family. He seems to have done so quite without inhibitions, and the last act is evidently meant to be the climax. The star of Shakespeare's Globe Theatre, however, was a short man, easily out of breath, and so for a while all the heroes had to be short and easily out of breath: this went for Macbeth as well as Lear. As a result the plot was deepened for him: and probably by him, too. Cascades and rapids were built in. The play became so much more interesting: it looks as if they must have remodelled and readapted it on the stage as far as Act 4, then found themselves faced with the problem of how to bring this hesitant Hamlet up to the final ranting bloodbath that was the hit scene of the original play. Act 4 contains a number of scenes each of which represents one possible solution. The actor may have needed to use the whole lot; or perhaps he only needed one, and the rest were none the less included in the book. They seem like so many bright ideas.

ACTOR: I suppose the plays may have been made like films are now.

LITERARY ADVISER: Possibly. It must have been a really gifted writer who pinned them down in the book versions, though.

ACTOR: From what you've said I'd picture Shakespeare coming along with a fresh scene every day.

LITERARY ADVISER: Exactly. I feel they were experimenting. They were experimenting just as Galileo was experimenting in Florence at that time and Bacon in London. And so it is right to stage the plays in a spirit of experiment.

ACTOR: People think that's sacrilege.

LITERARY ADVISER: If it weren't for sacrilege the plays wouldn't exist.

ACTOR: But as soon as you alter them in any way you're accused of treating them as less than perfect.

LITERARY ADVISER: That's simply a mistaken idea of perfection.

PHILOSOPHER: The Globe Theatre's experiments and Galileo's experiments and Galileo's experiments in treating the globe itself in a new

ABOVE
The German playwright believed that 'We are at one and the same time fathers of a new period and sons of an old one'

way both reflected certain global transformations. The bourgeoisie was taking its first hesitant footsteps. Shakespeare could never have tailored the part to fit that short-winded character actor of his if the feudal family hadn't just collapsed. Hamlet's new bourgeois way of thinking is part of Hamlet's sickness. His experiments lead straight to disaster.

LITERARY ADVISER: Not straight. Zigzag.

PHILOSOPHER: All right: zigzag. In a sense the play has the permanence of something makeshift, and I agree that that probably has to be resolved if we're to preserve it.

LITERARY ADVISER: Have we got to scrap all those marvellous old plays?

PHILOSOPHER: I wouldn't say so.

ACTOR: What about *King Lear*?

PHILOSOPHER: It's partly a report on the way people lived together in a previous age. All you've got to do is put the report into effect.

LITERARY ADVISER: A lot of people think such plays ought to be performed as they stand, and claim that it would be barbarism to make any change in them.

PHILOSOPHER: But it's a barbaric play. Of course you need to go about it very carefully if you're not to spoil its beauty. If you're going to perform it on the new principle so that the audience doesn't feel completely identified with this king, then you can stage very nearly the whole play, with minor additions to encourage the audience to keep their heads. What you cannot have is the audience, including those who happen to be servants themselves, taking Lear's side to such an extent that they applaud when a servant gets beaten for carrying out his mistress's orders as happens in Act 1, scene 4.

ACTOR: How are you to stop it?

LITERARY ADVISER: Say he was beaten and injured, then staggered out with every sign of having been hurt. That would change their attitude.

ACTOR: Then you'd have people turning against Lear for reasons associated with purely modern times.

LITERARY ADVISER: Not if you're consequential about it. The servants of this generally unwanted king could be

As soon as you alter the PLAYS in any way you're ACCUSED of treating them as less than PERFECT

BERTOLT BRECHT

shown as a little group which no longer gets its meals anywhere and pursues him with dumb reproaches. Lear would have to wince at the sight of them, and that would be a good enough reason for him to lose his temper. You just have to show the feudal conditions.

ACTOR: In that case you might as well take this division of his kingdom seriously and have an actual map torn up in the first scene. Lear could hand the pieces to his daughters in the hope of ensuring their love that way. He could take the third piece, the one meant for Cordelia, and tear that across once again to distribute to the others. That would be a particularly good way of making the audience stop and think.

LITERARY ADVISER: But you'd destroy the play, because you'd be starting something that led nowhere.

PHILOSOPHER: Perhaps it does lead somewhere; we'd have to look at the play. In any case it wouldn't hurt if there were some abnormal episodes of this sort, hotbeds of inconsistency that one suddenly stumbled into. The old reports are full of such things. It's already impossible to perform these medieval plays to audiences that don't have any historical sense. That's sheer folly. But Shakespeare is a great realist, and I think he'd stand the test. He always shovels a lot of raw

material on to the stage, unvarnished representations of what he has seen. And there are those useful junction points in his works where the new in his period collided with the old. We, too, are at one and the same time fathers of a new period and sons of an old one; we understand a great deal of the remote past and can still share once overwhelming feelings which were stimulated on a grand scale. And the society in which we live is a very complex one, too. Man is the sum of all the social conditions prevailing at every time, as the [Marxist] classics have it. All the same, there is a lot in these works that is dead, distorted and empty. This can continue to be printed: for all we know it may be shamming dead, and it may anyway explain other aspects of this past period. I would almost sooner draw your attention to the wealth of living elements still to be found in such works at apparently dead junctures. An infinitesimal addition, and they spin to life, specifically now, specifically not till now. What really matters is to play these old works historically, which means setting them in powerful contrast to our own time. For it is only against the background of our time that their shape emerges as an old shape, and without this background I doubt if they could have any shape at all. ∎

Sonnet 130

My mistress' eyes are nothing like the sun;
Coral is far more red than her lips' red;
If snow be white, why then her breasts are dun;
If hairs be wires, black wires grow on her head.
I have seen roses damasked, red and white,
But no such roses see I in her cheeks;
And in some perfumes is there more delight
Than in the breath that from my mistress reeks.

I love to hear her speak, yet well I know
That music hath a far more pleasing sound;
I grant I never saw a goddess go;
My mistress when she walks treads on the ground.
And yet, by heaven, I think my love as rare
As any she belied with false compare.

ILLUSTRATION: VALENTINA VERC

*Sonnet 130 delights in travestying the usual clichés of love poetry, and the beloved "mistress" it describes is no
paragon of perfection. The last line sums up all that rot about roses, perfumes, music and goddesses as "false compare" –
and the compliment is made all the more powerful for being paid directly and without such embellishments.
While the poem's mistress is plainly "rare", the poem itself is wonderfully wrought. Try reading it out loud to
appreciate its rhetorical dynamism and copious little verbal effects. . . .*